CW01084395

AGNES MOOREHEAD

A VERY PRIVATE PERSON

by
Dr. Warren Sherk

[handwritten inscription: To Russell & Pam for unforgettable hospitality and fellowship. Happy Reading, John Warren & Jean Sherk 1-18-81]

Dorrance & Company   •   *Philadelphia*

ACKNOWLEDGMENTS

The author wishes to thank the following for their permission to reprint the material listed below.

GUIDEPOSTS — for "My Favorite Script" by Agnes Moorehead (*Guideposts*, August 1965).

GEORGE CUTTINGHAM, DIRECTOR, AMERICAN ACADEMY OF DRAMATIC ARTS — for material from *Charles Jehlinger, In Rehearsal* (AADA, © 1968).

To my wife
Jean

Contents

Preface

It was my good fortune to know the late Agnes Moorehead for quite a few years. We held many conversations in her beautiful home, mainly about religion and Americanism. Whenever I was in Los Angeles on business and her work schedule prevented us from meeting, we held long visits on the phone.

This book is not a definitive biography. It is a selective biography. Through the years as I came to know her better I realized what a very private person Agnes was. Because our relationship was along idea lines, it has been an adventure to discover how broad her entertainment outreach was.

The cooperation of everyone as I researched the parts of her life I was unfamiliar with has been an inspiration. People who didn't even know me often came some distances to meet with me for discussion. Others generously allowed me to penetrate their busy schedules.

It has been a labor of love throughout the long researching, whether on East or West Coast. My motive was well expressed by Fred Carmichael of Vermont and New York: "If you can catch an iota of the inspiration Agnes was to all of us who worked with her, then you have done a Herculean feat."

My thanks to everyone for being so kind and helpful in the preparation of this book. I sincerely hope as we explore her tremendous versatility in the broad fields of the entertainment media that we will come to better understand the philosophy of her craftsmanship, her personal faith, and her dedicated Americanism.

My reason for keeping this book selective is because I have

tried to bring the reader as broad a picture as possible without revealing Agnes definitively. Why? I wish to respect her private life because she was a very private person.

Castle Hot Springs, Arizona
December, 1975

Acknowledgements————

California

    Polly Garland
    Freddie Jones
    Franklin Rohner
    Cesar Romero
    Paul Gregory
    Hans Conried
    Ruth Warrick
    Jim Jacobsen
    Mrs. Rhys (Elsie) Williams
    Joseph Cotten
    Lucille Ball

New York

    Harold Teichman
    John Houseman
    Charles Raison
    Ruth Neuman
    Elizabeth Crafts
    Fred Carmichael
    Sister Marie Davis
    Hans Conried
    Ruth Warrick
    Polly Bergen

Michigan

    Charles Gershensen

Vermont

    Fred Carmichael

Ohio

    Margery and Vic Stover

New Jersey

    Mary Roebling

Arizona

    Mrs. Ray Stout
    Barry Nouhava
    Richard Stacy
    Judge William Eubank
    Hardy Price

Tanya Hills
Edward Mulhare
Ricardo Montalban
Geraldine L. Page
Jan Bartram
Barbara Shook
Tempe Secretarial Service
Morenci Shepherd of the Hills Church

New Mexico

Charles and Betty Diebold

Part One

For   Freddie Jones and
Polly Garland

1

Tired into the Future

Orson Welles, Charles Laughton, and Paul Gregory were credited by Agnes as the three most influential men in her career.

Welles brought her to Hollywood in 1939 for the movie *Citizen Kane*. She appeared in sixty-five movies over the next twenty-five years.

It was Charles Laughton who encouraged her to go on tour with her "Fabulous Redhead" readings.

Paul Gregory produced the First Drama Quartette's *Don Juan in Hell*, starring Laughton, Boyer, Hardwicke, and Moorehead. Mr. Gregory also produced *Caine Mutiny* and many other great hits.

Since Welles was out of the country and Laughton was deceased, it was axiomatic for me to try to locate Gregory. He is married to Janet Gaynor and has homes in Hawaii, Mexico, and Palm Springs. We finally set up a meeting in Palm Springs.

Paul Gregory very graciously filled me in on various aspects of Agnes' career. He at once mentioned he wished she hadn't struggled with *Gigi*, which was to be her final role on the stage.

Gregory told me: "When I learned Agnes was in New York last January [1974], we arranged to have dinner at Twenty-One. As we came out, she said, 'Could we just walk up Fifth Avenue a bit?' It struck me as odd. Then she said, 'Paul, I'm never going to see you again.' I said, 'Do you know what it is?' In her characteristic strong but elusive manner, she shook her head from side to side.

"Very soon after that she entered the Mayo Clinic in Minnesota. Sure enough, we never saw each other again.

"Agnes didn't drink, you know, but she would take a touch of champagne on occasion. Her religious belief allowed her that indulgence since she liked to allow as how the Bible said Jesus took wine.

"That night before we left Twenty-One, we had a drink of champagne. She then teased me about calling Janet and me right after our wedding to please come to her home in Beverly Hills for a post-wedding supper. She said, 'It'll just be a small affair. You bring the drinks, though, since you know I won't be serving any.'

"We arrived with a few bottles, assuming it was to be a small affair. To our surprise there were about 110 there. We laughed as we recalled the occasion. We're not likely to see her kind again." He shook his head. "Never, never again."

Mr. Gregory kindly brought out a copy of Shaw's *Don Juan in Hell* that showed the original First Drama Quartette on the cover. As he lovingly gazed at it, he said, "Do you realize they toured eighty weeks in that vehicle? What a trouper Agnes was! She was indefatigable."

When he mentioned *Gigi* again, I told him of my interview with Cesar Romero, who had long known Agnes and often squired her to various film colony functions. I mentioned that Romero, too, was sad that she had toured with *Gigi*.

Romero told me: "We talked often during the final months of what was to be her hardest show tour. She was so strong willed, but even Agnes began to wilt from the endless rehearsals and the gruelling touring. I'll never forget one night on the phone when I asked her how she felt. She said, 'I'm tired into the future.' That wasn't like Agnes at all. Not at all."

On one of my research trips to New York City, I learned through old friend Hans Conried that Ruth Warrick, also in the cast of *Irene*, had played the wife of Orson Welles in Citizen Kane. It was arranged for me to see Miss Warrick after a matinee of *Irene*. Jane Powell was the leading lady in that particular production.

To my immense surprise, when I asked Ruth Warrick if she

4

had seen Agnes last winter, she replied, "Of course. We had a party for the combined casts of *Irene* and *Gigi* at my apartment."

I asked her if by any chance she had a picture of Agnes. "Isn't that strange you should ask that? I just came across one the other day that must have been one of the last ones—if not the last one—taken before she entered the clinic."

"May I have a copy if you can relocate it?" I asked.

"Of course. Can you come by again tomorrow? I'll bring it with me then, just before the evening performance."

It seems I ought to mention here some bewitching experiences through the months of research. I never knew Ruth Warrick before. No one had even told me to see her. I called Hans Conried because I was wondering how he was doing after a long winter illness. He introduced me to Miss Warrick and I thereby received the coveted recent picture of Agnes.

On another trip to New York, the director of the American Academy of Dramatic Arts, Charles Raison, put me in touch with a person who had known Agnes at AADA fifty years before. The moment I spoke to her on the phone to ask if she recalled Agnes, she replied, "Oh, yes, we called her 'Bobby.' "

I said, "I never knew she had a nickname." I had never encountered it in thousands of letters, wires, notes, mementos. Yet suddenly, out of the past, here was a voice telling me of her nickname. It was bewitching!

On the next trip to Beverly Hills, I mentioned the nickname to Freddie Jones, her housekeeper of many years. She couldn't believe it either. At first she acted like she was shot or had seen a ghost. She put her hand to her throat and said, "Where did you hear that name?"

I explained.

She sighed and said, "We found a trunk with that name on it in the garage. We had absolutely no idea where it had come from or who Bobby was, as Miss Moorehead had never mentioned it to us in living here over twenty years." I call that bewitched.

Just recently I decided to check back with Joseph Cotten to

see if he had located an old picture of Agnes that he thought was very chic. The day I phoned he said, "I just located it yesterday. Funny thing you should call today. Where are you?" I explained. He kindly said, "If you can come right over, I'll get the picture for you."

Repeatedly while I was researching, I'd pick up a book at random in a hotel, motel, or airport bookstore and quite often I'd run across something about Agnes or relating to her past. It was always something no one had previously mentioned to me.

2
Near the End

Nineteen seventy-three was drawing to a close. For the second straight year, Agnes was to miss her favorite annual Christmas party at Villa Agnese, her lovely home in Beverly Hills. Her farm in Ohio was managed by the Stovers. She wrote the Stovers on December 10, 1973 [most probably from New York City]:

> What a lovely cyclamen plant. It is just beautiful.
> Thank you for remembering this tired, weary traveler who longs for home and fireside.
> May the holidays bring you great joy, and the New Year a fulfillment of all your dreams.
> Love to all—
> Always
Agnes Moorehead

Again at Christmas, 1973, she wrote the Stovers:

What a beautiful collection of gifts! The bag [lilac tote] is divine and matches perfectly my other luggage. The soap is almost too pretty to use, and you *know* how much the prayers mean to me. [*Prayers of Peter Marshall*] This beautiful book will be with me always, for I shall treasure it. You are all so good to remember me, to make my Christmas a really memorable one. Thank you, and may the New Year fulfill all your dreams.

Love,

Agnes

January, 1974 [from Mayo Clinic]

Dear Stovers: Vic Sr., Margery, Vic Jr., Holly, Kathy, Heidi & Heather—

A short note to tell you how much I appreciate all the messages on that pretty decorated paper [violet].

Somehow you all make me homesick telling me about the snow and the deer. I love and miss this kind of life, the good clean fresh air of the country and hope one day I, too, will be able to settle down to having my fill of it. Meanwhile it does my heart good to know you are enjoying it.

With every good wish—

Always

Agnes Moorehead

Margery Stover said: "Thought you might like these letters, to see no matter how busy or ill, she could still find time to say thank you.

"I thought of some other things after you left that I meant to tell you. Remember how we said we tied a yellow ribbon 'round the old oak tree at the Lane's entrance to New Place? I meant also to tell you that the children would always make big Welcome Home signs and hang them with streamers all over the kitchen.

"Kathy is our artist and always drew Agnes some farm pictures, which would be propped up against the sugar bowl. The last get well card the children sent was a drawing of Bruno with an original poem by Kathy that went:

A get well card on a wonderful day
When the fields are full of clover and hay
And even though I'm far away
I think of you in every way.

Love,
Kathy

On a beautiful warm spring morning
The sun will shine warm on you,
And Jesus will send his blessing
Because you are kind and true.

Love,
Holly, Heidi and Heather

"Agnes thought it so cute, her letter said in part, 'Kathy's lovely color sketch was especially pleasing for its picture is close to my heart. The poetry was delightful and very good coming from one so young.' "

My mind went back to the interview with Cesar Romero when he recalled their last conversations. It made him reminisce.

Romero had said: "I wish she had never gone into production of *Gigi*. She began with it in San Francisco in July, 1973. Courageously stayed with it until December in New York City where she left the cast.

"She was a compulsive worker—very much admired by her peers. We only made one movie together, something Warner Brothers put out called the Story of Mankind. She was Queen

Elizabeth, as I recall. I was a Spanish nobleman, and Reggie Gardiner was Shakespeare."

I asked Mr. Romero about his fine collection of elephants. "Oh, yes, I've collected the elephants since 1952. In fact, Agnes' last gift to me was a beautiful silver Cambodian elephant the Christmas of '73.

"You've certainly learned what a trouper she was! I recall her telling me of performing her one-nighters in Israel." He paused and looked out the window across the distant lawn. "Agnes was probably the last of the great ladies of the stage to travel so far, so often, and so much.

"Did she ever tell you about our trip to Duluth?" I nodded that I seemed to recall her mentioning it once. "We were supposed to conduct a one-night show for some sort of a high school reunion. Instead of one show for 2500 persons, we had to perform *three* times for the over 8000 that turned out, totally unpredicted. What a night! I shall never forget it. This led Agnes to say in one of her inimitable ways, 'Never have so few labored for so many for so little.'

"When you think of Agnes, you think of perfectionism. She loved beautiful things. But she never got to see her house repainted and redecorated because her last illness took her first.

"Did you ever know about her aid to the Sybil Brand Institute? Among her other endeavors she was instrumental in helping get the new Los Angeles City Jail for Women.

"She was a self-made woman, just like one hears about the proverbial self-made man. Everything she had she earned herself. I felt sometimes she had an almost obsessive fear that she would not ever have enough to live on. Her pride in her craftsmanship, her religion, and work drove her. She wanted to be totally independent.

"The night she won the Emmy Award she just sat there stunned. She was totally unprepared to accept. She said, 'I've never won before, so I expected I wouldn't this time. I wish I'd have dressed for it.' She just sat there, too stunned to move. I said, 'Agnes, Agnes—get up, get up, go up and accept it.' "

I observed that through all the personal memos I had scanned, she was so private that I found little or nothing truly revealing about this fascinating lady. I mentioned again to Mr. Romero that all my conversations with her were attuned to philosophical discussions about either religion, Americanism, or her craftsmanship.

Fred Carmichael related: "I first met Agnes at the Nashville Airport when she came down to film *Dear Dead Delilah* with Will Geer, Michael Ansara, and my wife, Pat Carmichael. The first awesome appearance of the woman we were to come to love as 'Little Missy' soon gave away when she was chatting with a sailor who had sat next to her on the plane, and was signing an autograph for his younger sister while awaiting the luggage [lavender, of course!].

"The seven weeks we spent filming in early 1972 had Agnes darting back and forth to the West Coast and moonlighting between *Bewitched* segments in order to be with us. She would phone me one day and say she could be on such and such a flight and would be able to stay three or four days. And she would add that if I met her at the plane, allowed a half hour to the mansion where we were shooting, she could be in makeup immediately and work through the night if necessary. What a trouper she was! Words can never capture her almost desperate desire for perfection and total dedication to her craftsmanship.

"Since you have indicated you are heading towards the more inspirational aspects of people's relations with Agnes, I shall try to keep to them. We had a marvelous long ten hours once, when I drove her to her Ohio farm and we kept awake by relating our life's stories to each other. She had a kitten on her lap—a stray, which she would give a home to on the farm. The rain poured solidly all night, but we had a wonderful time.

"Her mother was visiting at the farm and had homemade sugar cookies and hot tea for us when we arrived. I promptly came down with the 24-hour flu and was bedded in Agnes' bed, and she brought me tea and medications.

"She jokingly said that if I told the folks in Vermont that I

10

had slept in Agnes Moorehead's bed, I better add that she had bunked in with her mother. Of her farm, Agnes said, 'Here I could hide away with a cup of tea, an apple, a good book and let the world pass by.'

"You probably know of her fondness for trains and that she loathed airplanes, always sitting on the aisle seat so she would not have to look out the window.

"Evidently her parents were very important in her life. Her description of how her mother told of her father's passing was really lovely. It seems that her father passed away at church and Mrs. Moorehead was sure that she saw his very spirit leave the body and seem to ascend from it.

"Agnes was always deeply indebted to her mother for 'playing along with me' when she was young. She had such strong imagination. She would come downstairs some mornings and her mother would say, 'Good morning, Agnes,' and Agnes would say, 'I am not Agnes this morning. I am Cynthia and Cynthia is sad.' Then Agnes would relate how she would stare out the window with tears rolling down her face. If a neighbor were to chance by and ask her mother what was the matter with Agnes, her mother—keeping up the game—would answer, 'That isn't Agnes, it is Cynthia and Cynthia is very sad this morning.'

"Agnes really knew that this strange kind of encouragement (or lack of discouragement) was a great help in undergirding her. She was often to mention how her father would play along with her when she loved to mimic people walking along the streets and he would always enter into the imaginative game with her. [Discouragement of the young at this point is far more prevalent than many parents realize, until it is too late.]

"One night during filming *Dear Dead Delilah*, we were all gathered in the library of the estate location between shots when the juvenile in the cast came in with a broken arm (which had not happened during filming sequences). Agnes told him how silly he was to risk himself so when he had signed to do a film and 'belonged to the producer and owed it to the producer to take care of himself.' Then she launched into a long speech on the meaning of craftsmanship in our business and what the actor ought to do about it and what he should bring to it. As Pat (my wife) and I have often said, we should have had her totally impromptu speech recorded and play it for each young actor whenever they came for an audition or interview. It was glorious. She had such a respect and love for the business!

"One night we had been shooting for twenty-one straight hours (with meal breaks, of course) in evening clothes and finally were down to the close-ups, and I told Agnes I would take her back to the hotel, but she said she would stay and read in the lines for Pat's close-ups as it might help her rather than hearing someone else read them in. That was being a trouper in the old-fashioned sense of the word—after twenty-one straight hours of working!

"The last scene of Agnes that we shot was her death scene (ironically for a movie that the last *was* last—not usually filmed that way for obvious production reasons). In it she collapsed after firing a gun and saving Pat's life at the hands of the murderer. They took some of the scenes and then wanted another angle. It was getting on to 10 P.M. and then we were going to leave for the farm afterwards. Between takes, I asked her if she wouldn't like to go to the trailer and rest, but she said she would stay stretched out in the cold on the brick path as it would waste time to have to get her back into the same position where she had fallen after shooting the murderer. It was a sight to see her lying there with all the folds of the long chiffon dress in the same neat position of the last film shot. So we chatted and exchanged stories, and as always she topped me. They suddenly yelled 'Action.' Her face that had been joking went down and her eyes filled with tears. She said her speech and they said, 'That's it. Cut.' Agnes said, 'So be it—let's go to the farm.'

"Whenever she was on the set, there was such respect. She seemed to demand it by her very presence more than anything else. The 'grips' would stop swearing when she appeared—once when I brought her onto the set and they were ripping off four-letter words, she gave a quiet 'shhh' and that was it.

"First and foremost there was a delicious sense of humor, one I did not expect from a lady (as I often told her) who had scared me all through high school by glaring at Greer Garson in one of her many cinematic films. Her stories and her ways of telling them were always gems in themselves and hilarious. I don't think she was ever allowed the chance to exhibit this as much in her roles as she might have been. At one luncheon, the manager of the tiny tea room near some antique shops had asked her if anyone had ever taken her for Endora the witch in *Bewitched*, and she said, 'Yes, I was, and would you like to be turned into a frog?' He literally backed out of the kitchen and was not seen again. A waitress took over from there.

"I often asked when she was going to take a rest, and she said she would but she should work while she could and in as many different type roles as possible or they would say next spring, 'Who is Agnes Moorehead?'

"On subsequent trips to New York, when she was in plays, or just visiting, we would get together for dinner, the theater, and always it was the height of the evening to listen to her recall and recount how she got her first role, job hunting, and of the three great men in her career life, Orson Welles, Charles Laughton, and Paul Gregory. Her talks of the people she worked with were all the more remarkable because there was never anything vindictive. If she ever did say anything the least bit negative, she would omit their names, and believe it or not, in our presence anyway, this only happened twice.

"Backstage at *Don Juan* in New York and again the next year with *Gigi*, she was just marvelous and evidently appreciated one's opening-night gifts, thoughts, memos, and other mementos. *Gigi* was an unhappy experience for her from first to last, and it will ever be an unhappy thing for me that it didn't turn out the way it should have—I mean the production.

"I just thought of a marvelous scene that comes to mind at the farm. Mrs. Moorehead told Agnes that she had just seen her in a rerun on TV of *The Left Hand of God*, and that, 'Really, Agnes, you were very good.' I replied that was a foregone conclusion with so many Oscar and Emmy nominations. Then Mrs. Moorehead went on to say she never had seen all of Agnes' films because she had made so many. Then Mrs. M. pulled out a local paper with an article about herself entitled 'Your Neighbors and What They Do.' It had a sub headline 'Mother of Star Kept Busy'—this is not a direct quote, but from memory. It just showed how Agnes was intent not only on her own press clippings, reviews, and such, but was even interested in her mother's, and her mother's opinion of Agnes' theatrical work.

"*Delilah* has been released in the Midwest and South through some chains, but now is back with the producer and will be recut and then released again—we hope. It is a horror film, more or less, but with some character to it. She plays a dying scion of a family.

"Probably one of the nicest things Agnes ever said to me was once when she said, 'But you are a gentleman,' and that sums her up marvelously. She was ever a lady and liked to be treated like one. I shall always keep the treasured photo signed by her with Pat's and my name from 'Little Missy.' She was a great lady, on and off the stage.

"Did you know that she cut her hair for the part she played of the plain pioneer wife to Karl Malden in *How the West Was Won*? She didn't have to do it, but she told someone who persisted in calling her *Agg-a-ness* on the set that she was just too hot—so she cut it, her beautiful long red hair. They told her that there were underwater skin divers specially equipped so as to save anyone if they fell off the pioneer rafts during the filming of the movie. Her reply, 'Humpf, fat chance they'd find me if I was swept overboard.' "

I have mentioned several times that various interviewers told of Agnes liking to do imitations. Fred Carmichael said, "Several of us were astounded at her excellent imitation of Hermione Gingold in *A Little Night Music*."

While they were making the film *Dear Dead Delilah*, Agnes

once said to Fred Carmichael, "Those who work for the good of the production I'd do anything for, but those who work for themselves alone, they'll just have to look out for themselves."

After seeing and talking with many friends, acquaintances, and theatrical people, I left it to Fred Carmichael to enlighten me as to why Agnes never drove. Many mentioned that she always needed to be chauffeured. I supposed that perhaps she had never learned to drive. Not so.

Carmichael: "She was driving the lavender Thunderbird home from a set one evening when she became so deeply engrossed in thinking about a new character she was portraying that she drove by instinct until she 'came to' way down in a very undesirable part of Los Angeles. She had no idea how she got there. 'That did it,' she said to herself. 'I'll never trust myself behind the wheel again.' And, true to her word, she didn't. This was divulged during our all-night drive that time from filming *Delilah* as we drove her home to her farm."

That same night each was regaling the other (in order to keep awake on the long drive) with unusual persons they'd run across in their lifetime. Agnes mentioned that years before, she once had a cameraman on the set who was one-eyed. He was forever running out of film. She nicknamed him "Rembrandt." She told how she insisted they try to keep ahead of him by asking *if* he had enough film loaded. It could be very disconcerting.

One time in Nashville they were supposed to be at a horse farm outside the city to film at six o'clock in the morning. Agnes was eating a breakfast of melon and cottage cheese. She said to Fred, "You're early."

"I don't think so," he said. She looked at her watch and said, "OK, let's go." How many unfinished meals, how many unslept nights on tour, how many unfinished tasks just to be prompt, ready, *on time*?

With the ensuing events of President Nixon's resignation from the presidency, I am glad that Agnes was not around to suffer his resignation. She had a favorite picture in her living room taken at the garden at the summer White House at San Clemente when President and Mrs. Nixon entertained many old entertainment friends and acquaintances. Agnes received not one, but two, invitations to the 1972 inauguration. One was from the White House, the other was personally from President Nixon. They were dated November 30, 1972 and December 5, 1972. Here is another letter:

THE WHITE HOUSE

December 4, 1972

Dear Miss Moorehead:

As I look back to victory of November 7th, I realize how much I owe to those who with their talent and support helped us roll up a majority of landslide proportions.

I shall always be proud that so many from the entertainment world were willing to play a part in the campaign and I am especially grateful to you for your efforts.

You may rest assured that over the next four years I shall do everything possible to make a record which all Americans regardless of party, can view with pride as we are about to celebrate our nation's two hundredth birthday in 1976.

With appreciation and best wishes,

Sincerely,
Richard M. Nixon

One of her most esteemed friends was Mary Roebling, of Trenton, New Jersey, and New York City. Mrs. Roebling wrote me the following beautiful thoughts:

I find myself wondering, in these bitter-sweet days of retrospection now that a much loved friend, Agnes Moorehead, has left us to be with God, what were the special qualities that she possessed that endeared her equally to the intellectual sophisticate and to the innocent youngster.

Agnes was a great artist in the theatre, revered by her contemporaries for her enormous talents and rewarded with accolades and wealth by audiences worldwide. But that rare and special quality that Agnes possessed was that she was an artist in living. All her life Agnes sought to see improvement in every dimension in her life. To seek self-improvement, an individual has to believe in life which means believing in one's self. Montaigne said, "Of all the informatives we have, the most savage is to despise our being." By this definition, Agnes Moorehead is the model of the civilized human being, she served others, made the world a better place in which to live without sacrificing her own center, her own individuality. She had a talent for happiness, a cheerful disposition, which flowed from her absolute conviction in God and the goodness in life enabled her to endure suffering and illness with rare grace.

Despite her fame there was nothing pretentious about Agnes; she displayed the same ease and grace with the youngsters as she did with the elite of the world.

I would say that Agnes' great triumph was her humanity. I remember the time she came to Trenton from New York City for Christmas. She had been staying in my New York apartment during the rehearsal for *Gigi* since mid-October. She was very tired, but very brave. My daughter had a small party for her and I shall always remember how this great lady of the theatre spent most of her time entertaining the grandchildren, Bryn and Ryan Balderston, ages 6 and 7 respectively. The children were fascinated with Agnes and they hugged and kissed her, a great sight to see. Agnes had very little to eat and rested much, but smiled in delight at the children. The children were absolutely beside themselves and wanted Agnes to disappear as she did on television as Endora, the witch. With enormous solemnity, she told them she hadn't her magic with her and that she was very, very sorry. We all exchanged presents and Agnes loved opening hers.

Finally, it came time to depart. We all kissed for a Happy New Year and then Agnes went back to my apartment. She stayed there until her illness forced her to enter Mayo Clinic in Rochester.

Agnes Moorehead was a truly beautiful person. I am honored she was my good friend. Now she has gone and I can but echo the words of the poet: "Rarely, comest thou Spirit of Delight."

I was very fortunate to be able to speak with Ricardo Montalban and Edward Mulhare of the current cast of *Don Juan*. They were just starting tour and came through Arizona.

Tanya Hills was introduced to me by Montalban. She aided Myrna Loy in the cast as she had helped Agnes.

Mulhare told me: "The thing that impressed me most about Agnes when we toured with her in 1971-72 was her always very strict high professionalism." (I was touched by the compliments Mr. Mulhare paid Montalban regarding the previous night's performance.)

Montalban added: "On the night of the day she died, I was opening in *The King and I* at Los Angeles. I was apprehensive enough as it was. Just as I was to go on the stage, in the final throes of preparation, someone said to me, 'Isn't it terrible about Agnes?' 'What is terrible?' I asked. 'She died today, somewhere in the midwest.'

"I couldn't believe it. I returned to my dressing room to try to recover myself. Just as I entered it another party said to me,

'Do you realize you are using the same dressing room Agnes Moorehead used in *Gigi*?' That did it. I broke down.'' Richardo continued, "You see, Agnes was responsible for my being in the cast of *Don Juan in Hell*." Then he added, "When we closed the show in Los Angeles, our next stop in *The King and I* was San Francisco. I nearly fell over when the dressing room they gave me was Agnes's—again. How did I know? The lamp bulbs had all been painted lavender, her personal trademark, you know."

Very few persons knew, even among her friends, that Agnes was in the Clinic. She entered in January 1974. She left us on April 30, 1974. It was her expressed wish that her fatal illness not be disclosed. Thus she was ever a very private person to the end.

Part Two

For   *Paul Gregory*
          Frank Rohner

3

Preparations

There are large voids as to any public statements, whether in movie biographies or what, concerning Agnes' early life. We know she was born in Clinton, Massachusetts, in the first decade of this century. It is not clear from what I could learn whether her father moved from the Boston area to St. Louis and thence to Reedsburg, Wisconsin, or vice versa.

She was born Agnes Robertson Moorehead of Protestant Irish ancestry. Her father was a conservative Presbyterian minister. She early indicated a natural attraction to the stage, or at least to making singing appearances. There is one story that at age three, she made an appearance singing "The Lord Is in His Holy Temple." Another account says she sang "The Lord Is My Shepherd." Whichever, it showed her early proclivity for the stage. She is known to have loved to appear at annual picnics at the Ohio farm in which she did make-believe roles.

She was allowed to be one of a group of girls who formed part of the ballet of the St. Louis Municipal Opera Company. It is not clear when this occurred. What is known is that she graduated from Muskingum College, New Concord, Ohio, in 1923 with an A.B. degree. She taught English and public speaking briefly at Soldier's Grove, Wisconsin. (Soldier's Grove's chief claim to fame is having the dubious distinction of having been flooded annually each spring for nearly 125 years.)

Next she studied for her master's degree at the University of Wisconsin. Upon completing her M.A. work in drama and public speaking, she proceeded to New York City. She had promised her father, whom she adored, that she would get her formal education out of the way before proceeding with plans to become an actress.

Whenever anyone would question her about her seemingly natural ability of happiness and cheerfulness, she would reply: "I think I learned of the happiness of being with people from my father. He was so warm and outgoing. He did not believe in just being a Sunday morning preacher to the congregation. No, he went to their homes frequently and invited them to ours.

"Even as a little girl I shared in the social activities of my parents. No one else had ever been in show business. But when I told my father at an early age I intended to start dancing lessons and later enter training to be an actress, he said, 'If this is what gives you happiness, go ahead. What you learn is sure to give happiness to others.' He was a very understanding minister, especially for the times. 'But,' he added, 'please get your formal education first. That will keep everyone happy, too.' "

With her father's blessing she had attended Muskingum and Wisconsin. Now her long-dreamed-of hopes and aspirations were about to be fulfilled. She yearned to enter the American Academy of Dramatic Arts in New York City. She proceeded there and auditioned in August 1926.

It gave me the greatest joy to come into possession, quite bewitchingly, of her *original* audition report at AADA.

AGNES R. MOOREHEAD
AUDITION REPORT — AMERICAN ACADEMY
OF DRAMATIC ARTS

Date: August 14, 1926
Name: Agnes R. Moorehead
Address: 535 Denver Place, St. Louis, Mo.
Single
Age: 23
Height: 5-4
Weight: 116

1929—Agnes graduates from the American Academy of Dramatic Arts.

Coloring: Brunette
Proportions: Good
Physical Condition: Good
Personality: Good
Stage Presence: Good
Birthplace: Mass.
Nationality: Irish-Scotch-English
General Education: B.A. Muskingum College - Post Grad.
   Univ. of Wisconsin
Occupation: Teacher of Eng. and math - High School
Previous Training: College dramatic award
Stage Experience: Amateur
Voice: Good (somewhat nasal)
Pronunciation: Mid-west R
Memory:
Reading: Very intelligent
Spontaneity: Good
Versatility:
Characterization: Good
Distinction:
Pantomime: Good
Dramatic Instinct: Yes
Temperament: Mental-Nervous-Vital
Intelligence: Keen
Imitation:
Recitation: "Italian Dialect Recitation" - "Quality of Mercy" -
   "Barbara"
Imagination: Good

Individuality and promise of a positive personality. Has
promise.

                    Acceptable
                    C. J. (Charles Jehlinger)

Oct. 1927

Agnes entered AADA in the fall of 1927. There is no data I could locate on what she did until then. Through the aid of Charles Raison, director of AADA, I was able to contact Elizabeth Council Crafts, who was her roommate from 1927 to 1928 while both attended AADA.

Crafts: "As I recall, we moved around quite a bit that year. We lived at Barbizon for Women, The Mayflower, Central Park West, and I recall one place up on Riverside Drive. In those days, Agnes was called 'Bobby.' I don't recall why, but that is what everyone called her."

According to the Academy, Agnes had classes in pantomime, vocal training, stagecraft, makeup, costuming, dramatic analysis, and dramatic literature. Rosalind Russell was a fellow classmate both years. The Academy has always been a two-year school, but no one is allowed to advance automatically to the second year until voted upon by the faculty.

We know that she helped support herself while at AADA by teaching part-time at the Dalton School in New York City. She did other side jobs, too, to make ends meet.

In the main lobby of the Academy there are photos of famous graduates with appropriate comments written by each. Agnes' words by her photo read: "I have always followed the principles taught at AADA throughout my career and shall continue to follow them."

Among the famous graduates through the years were: Spencer Tracy, Garson Kanin, William Powell, Walter Abel, Jane Cowl, Lee Bowman, Sam Levene, Lauren Bacall, Pat O'Brien, and, of course, Roz Russell and Agnes.

The present building of the Academy was formerly a private women's club. Its name was Colony Club, not to be confused with a more famous club known by that name. The architect of the building was none other than the famous Stanford White.

A member of the AADA staff is Ruth Neuman. She told me: "My most memorable thoughts of Miss Moorehead were that she possessed *both* charm and command. In the theater one seldom finds both in the same person.

"Before coming to New York and the Academy to work, we lived by chance in Beverly Hills. One Sunday afternoon in the mid-fifties, I was pushing my three toddlers in a specially rigged tri-stroller. Who should suddenly appear on the walk but *the* Agnes Moorehead. Pulling herself up at suddenly being confronted with *three* babies in a stroller, she said in that imperious way she could command, 'What magnificent children,' and hastened right along without another word."

Charles Raison told me, "I recall a most significant occasion for me in my young life in the mid-sixties. Agnes was touring with Joseph Cotten and his wife, Patricia Medina, in the play *Prescription for Murder*. It was in Williamsport, Pennsylvania, where I was then directing a college playhouse. The members of the cast and myself went out to a post-performance supper. Thomas Mitchell, whom everyone present knew personally, had just died. We all talked until after three in the morning."

In her second year at the Academy, Agnes appeared in several plays. It was the academic year 1928-1929. The plays and playwrights were: *The Springboard*, by Alice Duer Miller; *The First Year*, by Frank Crane; *Captain Applejack*, by Walter Hackett; *Chinese Lou*, by Clare Kummer; and *The Last of Mrs. Cheyney*, by Fred Lansdale.

That Agnes followed the principles set forth by the Academy was very evident from her successes. Her professor who most impressed her was the renowned Charles Jehlinger, affectionately known as "Jelly," the same man who originally auditioned her. In 1946 Professor Jehlinger was honored for his forty-nine years of teaching at the Academy. On that occasion he said: "It's easy to spot ability, but ability is only one thing. They also need ambition and concentration. I never once predicted which of the students would positively attain success." Below are excerpts from actual notes of Jelly's classes kept by Eleanor Cody Gould. One can easily see the influence of Professor Jehlinger upon Agnes.

"As long as you only talk words and expect to fool an audience, you are an idiot."

"Keep the head cool and the heart warm."

"It is a fatal thing to utterly yield yourself to your director. It is equally fatal not to yield at all."

"Unless you develop as men and women you cannot develop as artists."

"Never go through a rehearsal mechanically. Always use your *creative* faculties."

"Unless you are using your creative faculties, you are not making progress."

"Stay in the scene. Don't drop out after a speech."

"Never break illusion."

"The secret of the whole thing is this: Yield to the character and let it take control of things."

"Simply obey simple rules simply."

"Don't blur your canvas with too many details [creativity again]."

"The first step is to be a good listener, a sensitive listener."

"The capacity to take infinite pains is the most intelligent definition of genius." [Agnes Moorehead did this.]

"You must not stiffen. You cannot play a piano with stiff fingers, neither can you play a character with a stiff brain. Whenever you tighten up—relax."

"Gold does not come out of the earth ready to go to Tiffany's to be made into jewelry. It must be made ready. So do not allow yourself to be discouraged."

"You can never be a great artist without a great spirit of unselfishness."

"These things are important for acting student: love of the work, enthusiasm, simplicity, breeding, culture, gentility, temperament, health, and unselfishness." [Agnes Moorehead was strong in each.]

"You must acquire poise, mastery of self, strength of will and command one's own forces." [Tanya's mention of being "strong."]

"Read biographies of great people." [Later you will read about Agnes' library.]

"If you want to draw all the good in a man out of him, like him, love him, do something for him. Your character will respond to the same treatment."

"The whole basis of acting is listening. You lie to your audience if you are not listening. Thinking of cues and stage business is not listening. Listening is listening."

"A good actor does not act. A bad actor acts. A good actor creates."

"The theater should be a temple to the actor, not a factory."

4
Radio

The early years after graduation from the Academy are somewhat hazy.

Piece by piece we learn that Agnes returned to New York City to appear briefly on Broadway in supporting roles of such vehicles as *Marco's Millions, Scarlet Pages, All the King's Men,* and *Candlelight.*

At this point in her public career, Agnes seemed destined to become involved in the rather new media of radio. Eventually she was to become one of radio's top actresses. She actually appeared in a total of over twenty-five successful series.

Her favorites were Philip Lord's *The Seth Parker Show* and Lionel Barrymore's *The Mayor of Our Town.* Speaking of Barrymore, she once said, "I never heard him complain, even though he often was in intense pain." (His illness required first a cane, then a wheelchair.)

I inquired once about Lionel Barrymore's autographed photo prominently displayed on one of her tables—one of her "treasured photos," she said. Enthusiastically she said in reference to the radio days, "Did you know that Barrymore had invented the overhead boom microphone for radio?" I replied negatively. "He got the idea, he said, while fishing."

Then I learned that Agnes was in Jack Benny's first radio show. In her continuing years in radio she was often to appear as the foil for Bob Hope, Ed Wynn, Fred Allen, Phil Baker, Garry Moore, and Milton Berle.

Agnes often said, "Radio was sensational training. One had to convey characterizations merely by thrusting one's voice and not by being visual."

Somewhere in the numerous vitas put out by movies and stage releases, it is mentioned that she began radio broadcasting in St. Louis in 1923-1924 as a singer over stations KSO and KMOX. That she was a pioneer radio performer we know. That she was a singer is less known. Yet she was to appear in several musicals including her final performances in *Gigi*. This would seem to prove out the old philosophical adage "The end is the beginning and the beginning is the end," inasmuch as she seems to have begun and ended her brilliant career with music.

She played the part of Marilly on *The Mayor of Our Town*. She was also with the NBC *Seth Parker Show* as of 1932. Seth, himself, wired her "Success" when she opened with his show on February 7, 1932. She played the part of the wacky maid in a comedy series entitled *The Adventures of Mr. Meek*.

No wonder she enjoyed reading mysteries. She was in the radio mystery series of Sherlock Holmes, Bulldog Drummond, and the *Orange Lantern*. She was the sinister Dragon Lady in *Terry and the Pirates* and portrayed Margo Lane in *The Shadow*.

She was Min Gump with young Jack Kelk portraying Chester Gump. She was Homer Brown's mother in *The Aldrich Family*, in which Jack Kelk again appeared. There are many past performers who remember Agnes, but few kept in touch with her for forty years as did Kelk.

Perhaps her versatility in radio led her to become so versatile in the entertainment media generally. By the end of her life she

31

had excelled in ten different entertainment media forms.

We know that she appeared in as many as six radio shows a day at the top of her radio career. She was Ma Hutchison in *Circus Life.* Other serials were: *Brenda, Dot and Will, Life Begins, Life Can Be Beautiful,* and *This Day Is Ours.*

Orson Welles asked her in the late thirties to become a regular on his famous CBS show, *Mercury Theater of the Air.* This is not to be confused with Orson Welles, John Houseman, and Joseph Cotten's legitimate stage productions then known simply as *The Mercury Theater.* This was to be one of her most fortuitous meetings, since we know she credited Orson Welles with being one of the three most influential men in her career life.

In radio's *Cavalcade of America* series by Dupont on NBC, Agnes starred as Ann Hutchinson (#235) on July 7, 1941. Dupont's #238 in the same excellent series saw her portraying Dr. Josephine Baker (Typhoid Mary) on August 4, 1941. Agnes was to become world famous as the only woman allowed to be the voice of Eleanor Roosevelt on the celebrated *March of Time,* and she also played Madame Chiang Kai Chek. (I tried to locate tapes of these early shows with the help of *Time* magazine assistants but was unsuccessful.)

Since her early years on Broadway and in radio coincided with the Great Depression, she often mentioned waiting on table, assisting as librarian, teaching in a private school—anything to keep the proverbial wolf from the door. Until she ultimately starred in a series, there was no certainty of regular income.

Her attorney, Mr. Frank Rohner, told me: "There is an anecdote about her early years of the Depression. She once confessed to me that the only time she ever appropriated anything was once when she was very hungry she took a bottle of milk from a nearby apartment door. When she was paid at her work, she put the money back with a note of apology beneath the door from which she borrowed the milk. To her surprise, thereafter, for quite some time, there was a quart of milk delivered to her regularly, each morning."

A recent newspaper story emanating from Tokyo reports that "old radio lives again." It is part of the Far East Network, which is beamed to 128,000 members of U.S. military and Government families in Japan and Okinawa. What caught my eye was the mention of the old series called *Suspense*. We know that Agnes portrayed several heroines as a guest star on this series.

Who will ever forget Agnes' most stirring radio role as the bedridden woman in Lucille Fletcher's *Sorry, Wrong Number*, originating in May 1943. It was often repeated by popular demand in subsequent years. In fact, Agnes held the record for radio's most repeat performances. She did it twenty-six different times. She made a recording of it, which was very successful. There is a story that Barbara Stanwyck listened to the album while on set for the movie *Sorry, Wrong Number*. (I found no positive verification of this, however.)

When Orson Welles decided to take part of his group to Hollywood in the summer season of 1939, Agnes was invited to move with them and play the part of the mother in *Citizen Kane*. This opened up a whole new career in the cinema.

5
Filmography

From 1941, when *Citizen Kane* was released, until 1966, there were very few years Agnes did not appear in a movie. Some years she was in several.

1941

Citizen Kane — Mercury-RKO. In a cast that included Orson

Welles and Joseph Cotten, Agnes gave a distinguished performance as Welles' mother. Ruth Warrick was his wife. Ray Collins (later Lt. Tragg of Perry Mason fame), Everett Sloane, and Paul Stewart were from the original Mercury Theater group.

1942

The Magnificent Ambersons—Mercury-RKO. Cast included Joseph Cotten, Delores Costello, Tim Holt, Anne Baxter, Ray Collins. As Aunt Fanny Minafer, Agnes won the New York Film Critics' Award and her first Oscar nomination. It was almost as if she was so inspired by Welles and Cotten that she went even beyond her utmost.

Journey into Fear—Mercury-RKO. Cast included Welles, Cotten, Delores DelRio, Ruth Warrick, and Everett Sloane. This time Agnes played the part of a wife. This mystery script was written by Joseph Cotten. (Welles had scripted the *Magnificent Ambersons* from Booth Tarkington's story.)

The Big Street—RKO Radio. Cast included Henry Fonda, Lucille Ball, Ray Collins, and others in play about a Damon Runyon character. Agnes was a wife again.

1943

The Youngest Profession—MGM. Large cast with guest stars such as Lana Turner, Greer Garson, Walter Pidgeon, Robert Taylor, and William Powell. Agnes was a governess in a light story about teen-ager fan clubs.

Government Girl—RKO Radio. Cast included Olivia deHavilland, Sonny Tufts, and Paul Stewart. Agnes was a society leader in a wartime housing shortage comedy.

1944

Jane Eyre—20th Century-Fox. Cast included Welles, Joan Fontaine, John Sutton, Henry Daniell, Margaret O'Brien, Peggy Ann Garner, and Elizabeth Taylor. Agnes was a cruel aunt.

Since You Went Away—Selznick-United Artists. Cast included

Claudette Colbert, Jennifer Jones, Joseph Cotten, Shirley Temple, Robert Walker, Keenan Wynn, Lionel Barrymore. A society leader part again for Agnes.

Dragon Seed—MGM. Cast included Katherine Hepburn, Walter Huston, Akim Tamiroff, Turhan Bey, Hurd Hatfield, J. Carroll Naish, Henry Travers. Pearl S. Buck's novel in which Agnes portrayed an unforgettable, weak, and nagging Chinese woman.

The Seventh Cross—MGM. Cast included Spencer Tracy, Signe Hasso, Hume Cronyn, Jessica Tandy. Agnes was not on the screen more than five minutes but made the seamstress who helped an escapee realistic and vivid.

Mrs. Parkington—MGM. Cast included Greer Garson, Walter Pidgeon, Edward Arnold, Cecil Kellaway, Gladys Cooper, Tom Drake, Dan Duryea, and a large cast. Agnes played a chic baroness role.

Tomorrow the World—United Artists. Cast included Frederic March, Betty Field, Skip Homeir, John Carroll. Agnes had a spinster sister role in this one.

The only time she was to outperform the record six movies in this one year would be in 1956, when she was to make seven films.

1945

Keep Your Powder Dry—MGM. Cast included Lana Turner, Laraine Day, Susan Peters, June Lockhart, Lee Patrick, Jess Barker. Agnes was a WAC commander.

Our Vines Have Tender Grapes—MGM. Cast included Edward G. Robinson, Margaret O'Brien, James Craig, and others. Agnes was O'Brien's mother in this tender, loving film.

Her Highness and the Bellboy—MGM. Cast included Hedy Lamarr, June Allyson, Robert Walker. She was Lamarr's chaperone in this one.

1947

Dark Passage—Warner Brothers. A Bogart-Bacall vehicle in which Agnes played the estranged girl friend of Bogart.

There was a color passion in this movie. I've often wondered if this could have nurtured her passion for lavender.

The Lost Moment — Universal-International. Cast included Susan Hayward, Robert Cummings, Eduardo Cinnelli. She was Miss Hayward's 105-year-old aunt. The makeup job is reputed to have taken four hours to apply and over one hour to remove. As usual, she gave an extraordinary portrayal.

1948

Summer Holiday — MGM. Cast included Mickey Rooney, Gloria DeHaven, Walter Huston, Frank Morgan, and a large cast. Another spinster role in another aunt part.

The Woman in White — Warner Brothers. Cast included Eleanor Parker, Alexis Smith, Sydney Greenstreet, Gig Young. Another mystery, another wife role. Agnes will be long remembered for a scene with Greenstreet (as his wife) in which her classical profile predominated. It wasn't easy to steal a scene from Greenstreet.

Stations West — RKO Radio. Cast included Dick Powell, Burl Ives. Would you believe she was a gold-mine owner in this one?

Johnny Belinda — Warner Brothers. Cast included Jane Wyman, Lew Ayres, Charles Bickford, Stephen McNally, and Jan Sterling. Not only an aunt role again, but the second Oscar nomination.

1949

The Stratton Story — MGM. Cast included James Stewart, June Allyson, Frank Morgan. She was Stewart's mother in this baseball story.

The Great Sinner — MGM. Cast included Gregory Peck, Ava Gardner, Ethel Barrymore, Frank Morgan, and a large cast. Agnes was a pawnshop owner.

Without Honor — United Artists. Laraine Day, Franchot Tone, Dane Clark, Bruce Bennett. Agnes played the wife of Tone. She so often played spinster aunts and society grande dames that moviegoers forget she played opposite many great male stars.

Caged—Warner Brothers. Cast included Eleanor Parker, Hope Emerson, Jan Sterling, Lee Patrick, Jane Darwell, and a large cast. Agnes played a women's prison warden here. She researched this one at Tehachapi Prison. Agnes loved to surprise co-workers with solid homework for a part.

1951

Fourteen Hours—20th Century-Fox. Cast included Paul Douglas, Richard Basehart, Barbara Bel Geddes, Grace Kelly, and others. Agnes played a mother role again.

Showboat—MGM. Cast included Kathryn Grayson, Howard Keel, Ava Gardner, Marge Champion, Gower Champion, Joe E. Brown. Agnes played the nagging wife of Captain Andy (played by Brown).

The Blue Veil—RKO Radio. Cast included Jane Wyman, Charles Laughton, Joan Blondell, Richard Carlson, Audrey Totter, Everett Sloane, Natalie Wood. Agnes played a wealthy society woman again. Laughton persuaded her to do *Don Juan in Hell* after this.

Adventures of Captain Fabian—Republic. Cast included Errol Flynn, Victor Francen, Micheline Presle. Agnes' role was that of a servant-companion in this run-of-the-mill flick about New Orleans.

1952

The Blazing Forest—Paramount Pictures. Cast included John Payne, William Demarest, Richard Arlen, Susan Morrow, Lynne Roberts. Agnes played a landowner here.

Captain Black Jack—Classic Pictures. Cast included George Sanders, Patricia Roc, Herbert Marshall. Agnes was a socialite again.

1953

The Story of Three Loves—MGM. Three-part film. The part Agnes played in was called *The Jealous Lover*, starring James

Mason and Moirer Shearer. Agnes was an aunt again. She gave her utmost even to bit parts, and here she exemplified dignity and exuded sympathy to the hilt.

Scandal at Scourie—MGM. Cast included Greer Garson, Walter Pidgeon, Rhys Williams. Agnes' first portrayal of a nun, in charge of orphans. Reunited with Garson and Pidgeon.

Main Street to Broadway—MGM. Very large cast, including Tallulah Bankhead, Shirley Booth, Rex Harrison, Ethel and Lionel Barrymore, Louis Calhern, Helen Hayes. Agnes played an agent in this attempt to film backstage life of the theater.

Those Redheads from Seattle—Paramount. Cast included Rhonda Fleming, Gene Barry, Teresa Brewer, Guy Mitchell, Jean Parker, and others. Agnes played the mother of four girls during the gold rush days. Her spitfire performance is a reminder that the Latin derivation of *Agnes* is *agni*, which means "fire." She was truly named.

1954

Magnificent Obsession—Universal-International. Cast included Jane Wyman, Rock Hudson, Barbara Rush, Otto Kreuger. This role earned Agnes her third Oscar nomination. Here she portrayed Wyman's nurse companion. They were really something together, as in *Johnny Belinda*. Once again, she did her research by observing hospital techniques. It served her and the movie well.

1955

Untamed—20th Century-Fox. Cast included Tyrone Power, Susan Hayward, Richard Egan, Rita Moreno, Hope Emerson. This was set at the time of the Boer War. She played the governess of Miss Hayward's children.

The Left Hand of God—20th Century-Fox. Cast included Humphrey Bogart, Gene Tierney, Lee J. Cobb, E. G. Marshall, Benson Fong. Agnes played the wife of a mission doctor.

All that Heaven Allows—Universal-International. Cast included Jane Wyman, Rock Hudson, Conrad Nagel, Gia Scala. Agnes was reunited with Miss Wyman, and once again played her trusted companion.

Meet Me in Las Vegas—MGM. Cast included Dan Dailey, Cyd Charisse, Paul Henried, Lena Horne, and a host of guest stars. Agnes played Dailey's mother.

The Conqueror—RKO Radio. Cast included John Wayne, Susan Hayward, Pedro Armendariz, Ted DeCorsia, Lee Van Cleef, Tomas Gomez. Would you believe she played the mother of Genghis Khan (played by Wayne)?

The Revolt of Mamie Stover—20th Century-Fox. Cast included Jane Russell, Richard Egan, Joan Leslie, and others. Agnes turned blond for this one, as the proprietress of a Hawaiian house of ill repute. This had to be her most unlikely part.

The Swan—MGM. Cast included Grace Kelly, Alec Guinness, Louis Jordan, Brian Aherne, Jessie Royce Landis. Agnes played a dowager queen—regal and imperial.

Pardners—Paramount. Cast included Jerry Lewis, Dean Martin, Lee Van Cleef, and others. Once again she was a blonde, once again a mother, this time of Jerry Lewis.

The Opposite Sex—MGM. Cast included June Allyson, Joan Collins, Ann Miller, Delores Gray, Ann Sheridan, Charlotte Greenwood, Carolyn Jones, Leslie Nielson, Sam Levene. Agnes was the divorcée in this remake of Clare Booth Luce's *The Women*.

This was Miss Moorehead's most prolific film year, inasmuch as seven were released in this one year. This marked her forty-sixth film.

Raintree County—MGM. Cast included Elizabeth Taylor, Montgomery Clift, Lee Marvin, Rhys Williams, and others. This celebrated novel of a love story included Agnes as Clift's mother.

The True Story of Jesse James—20th Century-Fox. Cast included Robert Wagner, Jeffrey Hunter, Hope Lange, John Carradine, and others. Agnes played a mother again, this time of the bandit.

Jeanne Eagels—Columbia. Cast included Kim Novak, Jeff Chandler, Murray Hamilton, and others. Agnes was the confidante drama coach in this biography of the ill-fated actress.

The Story of Mankind—Warner Brothers. A fanciful version of Hendrik Van Loon's book of the same title. A tremendous cast of stars, including Agnes' long-time friend, Cesar Romero. Agnes was Queen Elizabeth I in this opus. The painting of her in costume is now at the farm in Ohio.

1959

Night of the Quarter Moon—MGM. Cast included Julie London, Nat King Cole, Anna Kashfi, Dean Jones. Agnes was a socialite mother again. This time of John Drew Barrymore.

The Tempest—Paramount. Cast included Silvano Mangano, Van Heflin, Viveca Lindfors, Oscar Homolka, Finlay Currie. This was not the Shakespeare vehicle. Agnes played a wife again.

The Bat—Allied Artists. Cast included Vincent Price, John Sutton, and others. Agnes received co-star billing in this one, in which she played a writer leasing an old mansion.

1960

Pollyanna—Buena Vista. Cast included Hayley Mills, Jane Wyman, Richard Egan, Karl Malden, Nancy Olson, Adolphe Menjou, Donald Crisp. Agnes played the town hypochondriac.

1961

Twenty Plus Two—Allied Artists. Cast included Dina Merrill, David Jansen, Jeanne Crain, William Demarest. Agnes was a high society dowager again.

Bachelor in Paradise—MGM. Cast included Bob Hope, Lana Turner, Jim Hutton, Paula Prentiss, John McGiver. Agnes played a judge, with her own inimitable touches.

1962

Jessica—United Artists. Cast included Angie Dickinson, Maurice Chevalier, Sylva Koscina, and many others. Agnes was a grandmother in this one—sort of a modern day *Lysistrata.*

1963

How the West Was Won—MGM. Cast included Spencer Tracy, Henry Fonda, Carolyn Jones, Karl Malden, Debbie Reynolds, Carroll Baker, James Stewart and a cast of thousands. Agnes played the pioneer wife of Malden and the mother of Debbie and Carroll. One of the few pictures in which she appeared with her neighbor, James Stewart.

Who's Minding the Store?—Paramount. Cast included Jerry Lewis, Jill St. John, John McGiver, Ray Walston. Agnes played Jill's mother and the artistocratic department store owner. Jerry said on an autographed picture to Agnes that "she gave my picture class."

1964

Hush, Hush, Sweet Charlotte—20th Century-Fox. Cast included Bette Davis, Olivia deHaviland, Joseph Cotten, Cecil Kellaway, Mary Astor, Bruce Dern, Marianne Stewart. As the slovenly maid, Agnes was nominated again as best supporting actress—her fourth nomination. This time most were sure she'd win, but who could beat the death scene of her main competition (Lila Kedrova in *Zorba the Greek*).

1966

The Singing Nun—MGM. Cast included Debbie Reynolds, Greer Garson, Ricardo Montalban, Katherine Ross, Tom Drake. Agnes was later to suggest Ricardo Montalban as Don Juan in *Don Juan in Hell.* He credits her for his part on the tour.

In the hall stairway leading down to the rumpus room of Villa Agnese, there is a poster on the left wall depicting some of the films she made during the twenty-five-year period of 1941 to

1966. It shows only thirty-seven of the more than sixty films — there was not enough room to include every one.

Below is some miscellaneous information I gathered during research concerning some of her motion picture films:

The little-known Chivwit Indian tribe was used for filming of *The Conqueror*. It was directed by Dick Powell.

After filming *Dragon Seed*, she took a trip to the Orient. She was later to meet Pearl S. Buck at a supper given for Pearl Buck and Agnes by Mary Roebling.

Although mostly on tour with *Don Juan in Hell* from 1951 to 1955, she still managed to help turn out five motion pictures, including the role that earned her her third Oscar nomination. Tucked away in one of the numerous books in her private library there was a "call sheet" for *Magnificent Obsession*.

UNIVERSAL INTERNATIONAL	11th day of shooting
Picture MAGNIFICENT OBSESSION #1749	Director: D. Sirk
Shooting call: 9 a.m.	Date: Fri. Oct. 2, 1953
Cast:	On Set:
Jane Wyman	8:45 a.m.
Rock Hudson	8:45 A.M.
Agnes Moorehead	10:00 A.M.
Richard Cutting	8:45 A.M.
A total of 6 stand-ins plus	
48 painters, plumbers, technicians, camera and sound crews, elect., props.	

Once, while being interviewed as to why she sometimes played comedy when she was renowned for regal parts or old crone parts, Agnes replied, "That's just it. I never want to be typed." Then she recalled being in Bob Hope's *Bachelor in Paradise* as the woman judge. "He liked for us to improvise. I recalled seeing a judge use a swivel chair once, so we inserted a swivel chair on the set. As for looking over and under bifocals, I'd seen another judge do that, so we implemented it, too."

There has been mention of how she prepped for certain parts. It wasn't just hospitals and women's prisons that she observed. She used a chemical lab and an electronics lab for her homework when she thought it would be useful to her role.

Her major film participation of necessity ended with signing a contract as Endora in television's *Bewitched*. This is understandable. She would occasionally make a film for television thereafter.

I have cited some names in the review of her movie career out of nostalgia—Ray Collins (buried next to Stan Laurel in one of the Forest Lawn cemeteries), Lionel Barrymore, Robert Taylor, Robert Walker, Finlay Currie, Walter Huston, Turhan Bey, Cecil Kellaway, Rhys Williams, Louis Calhern, Jeff Chandler, Nat King Cole, Adolphe Menjou.

Agnes appeared with every major film studio. She gave supporting role status to every top actress and actor of the time. Disappointed at her never winning an Oscar in the nominee races, her friend, Paul Gregory, once said: "You are the trunk of the tree, Agnes. Like every great supporting actor or actress, the stars are the branches. They depend on you for support, nurture, and strength. Without you and your like, they are nothing. Just notice how ludicrous big name stars look either on stage or in films if they aren't given good supporting actors and actresses."

6
Villa Agnese

Somewhere about halfway through the sixty-five movies, Agnes was privileged to purchase the one-time home of music master Sigmund Romberg.

The graceful winding flagstone walk leads to a Mediterranean villa surrounded by towering trees and a multitude of high flowering plants and shrubs. A small ceramic insert plaque indicates that this is Villa Agnese. The entrance is a massive ancient Spanish oak door. Above the medieval door is an inlaid charming ceramic tile bouquet of violets, denoting the owner's favorite color and flower.

Stepping inside, one notes a zebra-skin rug on the floor of the high-ceilinged foyer, complete with clerestory windows two and a half stories high. Everywhere there are bric-a-brac mementoes of favorite pastimes and places. The medieval Spanish door has an outsized key and chain elaborately strung along its massive width. The peephole is genuine from an ancestral Mediterranean mansion.

The interior is cool and quiet. Even the barking of two French poodles in the inner patio does not disturb the calm. There is a serene air of permanence about the place. Anything added to or subtracted from the decor could not affect the feeling of solidity that prevails here.

Up a short flight of stairs to the left is the massive living room with twenty-foot-high beamed ceilings. A grand piano is almost lost in one corner. Large statuary with flower pots flank a great marble-topped table covered with pictures of movie star friends.

In another corner is a cluster of round French-style chairs and table. A grouping of very large comfortable sofas surround the marble fireplace at the end of the room. A gigantic but still exquisitely lacquered coffee table is between the sofas. Exotic pompons hang from each drawer in the secretary, buffet, and other furniture throughout the room.

A small den and library is entered from each side of the fireplace at the far end of the living room. A veranda and stairs descend outdoors to the terrace patio which is beyond the inner patio. This intimate den library has an antique harp with some broken strings, and an antique chair compliments it. The smaller fireplace in the den has smaller comfy sofas on each

The fireplace in the living room at Villa Agnese.

side. The library part of the den is replete with history books, and complete sets of great literature. One set outlines the history of the theater.

As one passes back through the engulfing silence of the great living room, one sees a lovely picture of the royal family of Monaco on one of the numerous sideboards, a smiling President Nixon greeting Miss Moorehead in the garden of the western White House, and antiques galore.

Stepping back into the foyer, one can then enter the formal dining room which is opposite the living room. There is a full-length oil portrait of Agnes on the far wall opposite the foyer entrance. The chinaware in the dining room is the equivalent of any royal or first family anywhere. The furniture is the finest without being elaborate. The serving rooms are beyond.

Off the foyer to the rear is the inner patio. Just to the right of the patio door is a descending winding stairway that leads through a small tunnel to the rumpus room. A heavy four-inch-thick cord laced through large rings serves as a railing along the steps to the lower story. Posters from past triumphs line the walls of the tunnellike staircase.

It was here in the main area of the rumpus room that I spent most of the time researching the book, trying to fill out some missing parts and years.

The rumpus room is less formal than its counterpart above; nevertheless, it has a black piano and companion black-lacquered harp, complete with matching chairs. Objets d'arts from world travels and bookshelves line the walls on three sides. There is slide paneling to cover much of the downstairs library shelves. The fourth wall is windowed and looks up into the inner patio.

Favorites in the fiction line of the lower library shelves are humor, mystery, and drama. However, there is a sprinkling of every conceivable type of reading material, including the inevitable religious books which occupied much of the reading time of the owner.

46

Beyond the rumpus room is a smaller room equivalent to the den library above. It served as a semioffice and storage room for theatrical memorabilia. Awards line every inch of space on all four walls. There is a small mirror-topped desk and the workaday items such as appointment books, heavily referenced professional books, class notes and drama notes of her students. There is even the theological seminary notes of her father. From this private office, Agnes could go up the short stairs to the terrace patio, which was her favorite place to lounge outdoors.

Freddie Jones, her trusted housekeeper of over twenty years, told me: "Miss Moorehead would retire to the terrace patio of a Sunday morning and stay out there all day sometimes, rarely coming in until dark. She would take her radio, her special religious cassettes and tapes, her Bible, and her current scripts. Lunch would be served out there when she wished. It was what she called her sancto sanctorum. It could be reached just beyond the inner patio through an arbor or from her veranda stairway or even from her private office."

Villa Agnese is in the shape of an elongated U, with the living room and dining room comprising the front long side of the U. The short side is the kitchen and serving rooms downstairs and the long stairway, clerestory, and small rooms upstairs. The back side of the long part of the U is parallel to the front side just beyond the inner patio. Housekeeping quarters are on the first floor, and the bedrooms are above. Beyond the inner patio, at the end of the back side of the villa, one approaches the gardens and the swimming pool. The latter is long and deep. At the far end of the pool is a Roman wall, and set in at the top center is a beautiful ceramic tile Madonna.

Whenever Agnes entertained with garden parties, there were all sorts of segregated alcoves completely aloof from the rest of the gardens, each with separate Roman and Greek statuary complimenting the outdoor furniture.

When one looks at the autographed pictures of Marcel Marceau and Jonathan Winters, one recalls the stars of stage, screen, television, and radio who came up her flagstone walk to visit her. Marceau and Winters were at a party she once gave in the mid-sixties. She said afterward that someone should have taped the proceedings and antics of "those two."

Winters wrote her on October 22, 1968:

> I can't begin to tell you what a joy you are to work with. As you well know, those long hours on a TV set are gruelling to all of us and your *patience* as a professional performer was certainly appreciated.
>
> As always, you gave a tremendous performance. I can't tell you how much I enjoyed doing the Halloween sketch with you.

Jonathan Winters also thanked her for doing an Indian benefit. Here is a copy of the telegram he sent her for a supper invitation after the benefit:

> HOW! Indian fans. Me invite you to big Pow Wow at Chasen's Tummy Tepee for much fire-water and yum-yum. We gonna pay honor to Great Chief, Stewart Udall, Secretary of Interior and his medicine man, Robert L. Bennet, Commissioner of U.S. Bureau of Indian Affairs. They come here from big lodge in Washington. Day is Tuesday, October 15th 6:30 after moon come up. You call on voice machine to Wigwam 565 and tell if you gonna come or not. Better not speak with forked tongue, either. If you make treaty with me, no break it like John Wayne does in magic pictures. Me thank.
>
> Jonathan Winters

On the lower level there are two beautifully decorated-under-plastic Christmas trees, mute testimony to the great parties she was famous for each December. Her scrapbooks contain hundreds of personal Christmas cards. Jerry Lewis sent the following greeting one year:

The best preacher is the heart
The best teacher is time.
The best book is the world
The best friend is God. — The Talmud.

Among the Christmas telegrams she kept was one from Bette Davis:

Merry Merry Merry Happy Happy Happy

Bette Davis

From Pickfair came greetings from Mary Pickford and Charles (Buddy) Rogers saying "Mary and I wish you LOVE, HEALTH, FUN, HAPPINESS."

Buddy

The Christmas cards and greetings are on every conceivable theme — classical, religious, historical, photographical. Among the most beautiful was a large Thai temple in color and the greeting was in Siamese.

Joan Crawford, Zsa Zsa Gabor, and many others thanked her for her touching notes to them. Kay Gable once penned: "Thanks for your beautiful Christmas parties which give me the spirit to get right on the Christmas path."

Because she was such a private person, it was not known that her annual Christmas party to launch the season was either on her birthday or on the Saturday closest to it. The annual parties became so famous that they were covered by Chicago, New York, and Palm Beach papers, as well as local and regional ones.

Two hundred twenty persons attended what proved to be her last Christmas party in 1971. She was touring on the road with the second group of *Don Juan in Hell* casts in 1972 and with *Gigi* in 1973.

Norma Lee Browning of the Chicago *Tribune* wrote December 7, 1971, in her Hollywood *Today* column:

Speaking of stars, what a shining contingent turned out for Agnes Moorehead's Happy Holiday Party at her fabulous home in Beverly Hills. Agnes is one of Hollywood's most superb hostesses. Her parties are out of the tradition of filmdom's golden era, complete with madrigal singers. The house was decorated like a winter wonderland both inside and out.

Among the wall-to-wall celebrities were the Jimmy Stewarts, the Henry Fondas, Fred McMurrays, Lucille Ball, Zsa Zsa Gabor, with daughter Franscesca, Steve Lawrences, Steve Allen, George Kennedy, Virginia Graham, George Maharis, Ann Miller — who looked absolutely smashing in long black velvet with white ruffled cuffs and jabot. Agnes looked gracious and regal.

Freddie Jones told me: "Miss Moorehead had a positive philosophy about being a hostess. She stood at the door each year and greeted each person when they arrived and as they left. She disliked people who ran parties, but one could never locate them. Her idea was to be at the door. She never strayed from her hostess spot. We brought her little goodies, but she stayed at her post like a sentinel."

Dorothy Manners' column:

It has always struck me as an anomaly that Agnes Moorehead, one of the most intellectual ladies of her profession, one of the best educated, four-time Oscar nominee, a TV Emmy award winner, a founder and charter member of the famed Mercury Theater Players, is also one of the most indefatigable partygoers in town.

If Cesar Romero is our leading Man About Town, the veteran and venerable Agnes Moorehead is our leading Lady About Town. It's easy to spot her vivid red hair and colorful caftans at frolics and elegant soirees in Beverly Hills and at beach weiner roasts put on by Debbie Reynolds' children and their friends.

Freddie Jones said: "Miss Moorehead almost had a mania about being hostess and about guests. She used to dislike the ones who rang the doorbell before her dress was zipped up and the ones who left so early it was almost insolent. She liked them to enjoy themselves. She kept herself handy, at the door so people would find her if they had a question or a need."

Polly Bergen was a next-door neighbor for many years. She wrote me:

I can only think of a couple of stories about Agnes because I have spent so much of my time in New York the last several years. She was a delicious lady with a lovely sense of humor and the first anecdote is one that she related to me. . . . It was at a time when she was appearing in the series, *Bewitched*, and my son was quite young at the time, about six or seven years old, if I remember correctly. He had been told by his older sister that a witch lived next door. This, of course, was extremely exciting to him, and he spent hours standing out on the sidewalk hoping to catch a glimpse. You must understand that he had absolutely no idea who Miss Moorehead was. As the story was told to me by Agnes, one morning her black housekeeper went out to pick up the morning newspaper at the very moment my son was on his way to school. He immediately rushed over to her and said, 'Miss Moorehead, I love witches more than anything and I hope you will let me come inside your house someday and see your magic broom!' The housekeeper very sweetly said she would be more than happy to do that and went back into the house. Peter proceeded to tell everyone that he had finally met a real witch.

The other incident took place when my husband and I were giving a very large party at our house, and by large, I mean about 200 people. At the time, I really did not know our neighbors, but I felt it would be safer to invite all of them so that the noise wouldn't bother anyone living

51

nearby. If I remember correctly, Agnes arrived with Cesar Romero looking her usual, marvelous self.

It was a massive garden party with a 19-piece orchestra and though it was a Saturday night, I obviously had not invited enough of the neighbors to cover the sound that was being generated by a 19-piece orchestra. By 10:30 the police started calling with complaints regarding the noise—by 11:30, the police themselves arrived at the door with a gentleman in his pajamas who was ready to make a citizen's arrest. At midnight, we moved all the guests plus the 19 musicians into the living room. Agnes watched all this with great amusement, and at 1 A.M. came over to me and said, 'I really must go home as the evening is getting quite late, but more importantly, I feel it my duty to go home in order to call the police and complain about the noise,' she said with that what-could-be-wicked-smile of hers.

This is really all I can offer in the way of anecdotes, except to say that I thought Agnes was a truly remarkable woman and enriched the lives of all the people who knew her.

7
Queen of the Road

The time was the early fifties. The event was Paul Gregory's production of *Don Juan in Hell,* by the First Drama Quartet. The cast: Charles Laughton, Charles Boyer, Sir Cedric Hardwicke, and Agnes Moorehead.

Across four seasons they toured with this vehicle, twenty weeks a season, which meant nearly five months on the road at

Paul Gregory's First Drama Quartette production of *Don Juan in Hell* on tour. The cast (left to right) included Charles Laughton, Charles Boyer, Agnes Moorehead, and Sir Cedric Harkwicke.

a stretch. Agnes said of the company: "It was like a finishing course in Shakespeare to be able to perform this play with the likes of Laughton, Boyer, and Hardwicke. Every night was a new experience. This seldom happens to an actor. If I never acted again, I'd be happy for having done this remarkable show. The gruff-seeming Laughton had a heart like pink plush. He directed us, Paul Gregory produced, and Hardwicke would tease me about 'one more freckle.' "

Agnes liked to recall that "the magic of acting is being able to get over an imaginary wall between the actor and the audience. That we accomplished this in our First Quartette was an unforgettable experience."

Paul Gregory furnished me with the following comments about the great quartette from an old flyer:

San Francisco—The theater is looking up in this old town judged by rousing reaction to this new twist in theatricals. There has never been anything like it and probably won't be—without the likes of Laughton, Boyer, Hardwicke and Moorehead. We salute a new kind of impresario. It is all magnificent, brilliant, theatrical performance.

Sacramento—A jam-packed house witnessed the most startling piece of theatrics ever afforded this city.

Salt Lake—Smashed all attendance records playing to nearly 12,000 people in four days. One is entranced and captivated as the spoken word becomes great music and all are enthralled by majestic movement of words rarely seen since the days of the Greek theater.

Memphis—Capacity audience thrilled by pure theater. Four great stars teamed to present exciting, thrilling, absorbing pure drama as ever enjoyed here—if ever.

Washington, D.C.—Capacity audience came out of curiosity with added lure of four star cast. They left dazzled by most provocative, fascinating, theatrical demonstration of this or any other season. Shaw is the real star though every one of the four stars walked off covered with individual glory.

Indianapolis—Impressive performance before 7000. Magnificent show by first drama quartette. Everybody had rip-roaring good time.

London—The large audience was keyed up to the rare theatrical occasion from the start. Four stars, in immaculate evening dress, played their way to success. It was an unforgettable spectacle. Through this Quartette, Shaw is himself again. The Quartette has done something remarkable for the cause of the theater by their bold, pioneering spirit in presenting this magnificent piece.

Manchester, England—It was up to the audience to join in. This they did and it was sheer delight. The relish with which Charles Laughton licked his lines and twisted and turned was the Laughton the world loves. Charles Boyer stopped the show with his magnificent performance. Agnes Moorehead was radiantly beautiful and displayed superb artistry. Hardwicke is brilliant.

What provoked these acclamations? A section excerpted from George Bernard Shaw's *Man and Superman*. It was not a play, but a reading. The First Quartette gave this more than a reading. They read from memory rather than from texts. Their imagination, daring, brilliance, integrity, dignity, midst informality, fired the audiences. With nothing but some simple music stands to hold their manuscripts and a few microphones, this startling theater burst upon unsuspecting audiences. Agnes was veritably bewitched with her part long before she was to ever appear as Endora the witch on *Bewitched*.

Of Paul Gregory, Agnes remarked: "He is a great force in the dynamic theater. He wants to give audiences the *best* he can. We need people like him in the theater."

Mr. Gregory's successes include *John Brown's Body*, with Judith Anderson, Raymond Massey, and the late Tyrone Power; *The Caine Mutiny*, with Henry Fonda, Lloyd Nolan, and John Hodiak; and *The Marriage-Go-Round*, with Charles Boyer and Claudette Colbert.

Gregory told me: "Agnes often said, 'Acting is hard work, like digging ditches or factory labor, but after it's over, nothing can ever feel like the emotion when the curtain comes down and you know you've done a good job.'

"Agnes wanted to do *Don Juan in Hell* because she said, 'There is so much garbage in the theater.' We always hit it off well because she knew she could depend on me. Agnes was the glue that held it together.

"In addition to the eighty weeks of *Don Juan in Hell* that we did across four seasons, and, incidentally she performed at least six times weekly even on the road, I convinced her with the aid of Charles Laughton to let me produce her in her one-nighters. At first we called them 'The Fabulous Redhead,' and later 'Come Closer and I'll Give You an Earful.' But, as she so often said because she was such a private person, 'Don't come too close.'

"One time when we were on tour in Omaha (I forget the show), a woman came up to her and said, 'Miss Moorehead, you were simply marvelous as Medea.' Drawing herself up to her fullest stature, Agnes said, 'Madam, I was not Medea.' The lady persisted, 'Oh, you're mistaken. You were Medea.' Reflecting about it, Agnes then replied, 'Madam, if you saw me as Medea, then to you I was Medea.'

"Once in some city or other her fresh dress did not arrive on time for the performance. Quick as anything Agnes said, 'Is there a spare drape somewhere?' We found a used velour drape, miraculously. She draped the velour about her. She summoned an extra stock of safety pins. Within minutes, would you believe it, with a ruffle about her neck, she looked absolutely divine with her flaming red hair. It was an incredible performance.

"She toured all over the U.S.A. in '60-'61 in *Prescription for Murder* with Joseph Cotten, Patricia Medina, Tom Mitchell, under my production, as also *Lord Pengo* and others."

Tucked away in one of her personal fan scrapbooks was this little poem, unsigned and undated. I presume it came from this period because of the reference to Dona Ana in *Don Juan in Hell*.

> To a lady we admire
>> We think you're swell
> As Dona Ana
>> In *Don Juan in Hell.*
>
> We wish you the best
>> For your success
> We wish for you
>> Health and happiness.
>
> You make many happy
>> With the work you do
> May all the joy you brought to us
>> Come back thrice to you.

On the same page with the above was a little note, probably written by someone that shared a dining room time with her: "Sitting across from you in the dining room has brightened my dreary day." No wonder Agnes was so aware of the importance of fans. From all her lonely trouping for on-tour plays and her fabulous one-night personal shows, she, too realized that even sitting in the same dining room could be an uplifting experience for some anonymous stranger. The little more and how much it is!

Agnes teamed with Paul Gregory in *Prescription for Murder, Pink Lady,* and *Lord Pengo.*

Here is the touring itinerary for *Prescription for Murder.* It should give some idea of the magnitude of her touring schedule.

This play, with Joseph Cotten, Patricia Medina, and Thomas Mitchell, opened at the Curran Theater in San Francisco, then continued to the following: Denver, Topeka, Kansas City, Missouri, Omaha, Des Moines, Sioux City, Minneapolis, Duluth, Fargo, Hibbing, Eau Claire, Madison, Rockford, Philadelphia, Williamsport, Raleigh, Charlotte, Greensboro, Lynchburg, Cleveland, Detroit, Toronto, St. Louis, Pensacola, New Orleans, Jacksonville, Orlando, Tampa, Miami, Norfolk, Baltimore, Hartford, Boston, Montreal, Ottawa, Syracuse, Binghamton, and many, many more. The tour opened January 15, 1962, and closed May 12. All in less than four months. What a trouper!

Joseph Cotten called her the "Queen of the Road." This is some compliment, coming from Mr. Cotten. I was fortunate to interview him after his annual return from their sojourn in England. They keep an apartment there and in West Hollywood. I mentioned to Mr. Cotten that Charles Raison, the dynamic young director of the American Academy of Dramatic Art in New York, recalled seeing their production of *Prescription for Murder* at Williamsport when he was in charge of a new theater there. Raison recalled that the troupe was grieved by the sudden decease of Thomas Mitchell. He had left the cast in Philadelphia, just prior to their Williamsport appearance.

Cotten recalled: "Oh, yes, I remember the incident well, because we were all so shocked by Mitchell's death that we sat up until all hours talking.

"You have probably learned that Agnes disliked sharing a dressing room with anyone. To our amazement, she had to do this with my wife, Pat Medina, at one of the theaters on this tour. They became such good friends that she overcame her reluctance to share a dressing room with someone. She was such a private person, wasn't she?

"Do you know why I call her 'Queen of the Road?' It was not because she traveled more often to more places than any American actress in memory, *but* she gave so much time to what we refer to as 'the dreary groups.' My goodness, she was

Agnes Moorehead in *Prescription for Murder.*

unbelievable in her compassion for others, even the dreariest! *And*, every place we'd go, we'd find we were merely the curtain raiser for Agnes. Everyone seemed to know her everywhere— even to the most outlying provinces. She was the *queen* of the road.

"She was always trying to improve people in the theater and improve on the theater. It was like a mission in life for her—she did it evangelically and even with apostolic zeal.

"Agnes Moorehead was the most disciplined actress we ever met. She was the hardest-working member of our profession.

"Did you know about her ability to mimic and imitate? Even Katie Hepburn loved to have Agnes imitate her. She (Katie) would laugh until she'd split.

"But the one that always floored us was her imitation of the Dusa, all in French, yet. We'll never see her likes again."

Mr. Cotten continues with what he said was one of his favorite anecdotes about Agnes. "She'd never wedge Angier Biddle Duke out of his protocol job. We were once guests of Admiral Cavanaugh at a famous naval yard. After spending several hours with him, she gaily bid him good-by with 'G'bye, Commander.' "

The marvelous veteran actor from scores of films stood up and paced to the picture window of their beautiful penthouse as if to recall something. Then he said, turning around as I'd seen him do in so many movies, "Would you believe that Agnes and Bette Davis actually coached me in southern dialect for my role in *Hush, Hush, Sweet Charlotte*? I was born in the South, but since Pat is English and I played so many English parts, Bette and Aggie actually assisted my diction in that particular movie." He paused, as if even he found it hard to believe. Then he said: "I mentioned to you a while ago that we often felt as if we were just the curtain raisers for Agnes. Well, one time in La Jolla she asked me to do a one-act play by Christopher Fry. I agreed. I thought I did rather well, and, lo and behold, she came bursting in afterward with her sensational readings of *The Fabulous Redhead* and, sure enough, we were just the curtain raisers. What an actress! What a lady!

"I did many films with Aggie. But I'll never forget her in *Since You Went Away.* Can you imagine that? Claudette Colbert, Jennifer Jones, Shirley Temple, Robert Walker, Keenan Wynn, Lionel Barrymore, and yet, I can't forget her terrific part in that—she was so chic and so bitchy. She never had starring roles—always supporting, but without her, many a picture just wouldn't have had it, if you know what I mean."

Being a movie buff all my life, I said, "I believe *Since You Went Away* was made in 1944, which is thirty years ago."

Mr. Cotten paused with those soulful eyes of his and meditative quizzical look and said: "Think of that! Thirty years, and I recall *her* part like we just ran through it yesterday."

Through the years, I was struck with Agnes' constant emphasis on the philosophy of her craftsmanship. She told me: "Today we have too much emphasis on the neurotic, which can, if we allow it to, make neurotic machines, robots of us all. We must look beyond the surface of human beings—everything below that surface is not ugly or corrupt.

"Theater and its true expression are vital and necessary to our way of life. An actor must breathe life into words from a printed page. Acting is sometimes like a sixty-five-year-old man I once met when I went back to college for a refresher course. Everyone talked theory and books. He wanted to know about the practical applications. That is what matters in acting, too."

There was a notice in one of her books she obviously felt highly of, about Paul Gregory flying to Paris with S. Behrman to sign Charles Boyer for the leading role in *Lord Pengo*. Rehearsals began August 7, 1972, and they opened November 19 in the Royale Theatre on Broadway. In this play, Boyer was a slick art collector who liked to con people. Agnes was his faithful yet critical secretary who lent pungency to her part of the dialogues. One critic said of Agnes in this vehicle, "Miss Moorehead played the part with all the artistry one has come to expect of this excellent artist." Henry Danielle, Cliff Hall, and Brian Bedford rounded out the cast of *Lord Pengo*.

Opening night notes, wires, and such received and kept by Agnes included:

"Knock em dead, luv. Joan Fontaine."
"Good luck and love tonight. Ann Sothern."
"You've won the West, now win the East. Love, Carroll Baker."

Other persons' memos included those from Roz Russell, Dore Schary, Leland Hayward, Polly Bergen, Kathryn Grayson, Bea Lillie.

Vincent Price penned a note to her after attending a performance with the then First Lady, Jackie Kennedy: "We were escorted by a total of 38 police and secret service. Attending anything with a First Lady is not relaxing."

From this same production she had saved a backstage note that read: "That I couldn't have known you better is a source of regret—because the little was a pleasure."

The Manchester *Guardian* said of her in this same production, "Why must she be wasted when she is one of few Broadway actresses capable of playing tragedy?"

I must have waded through hundreds of letters, notes, and messages from this one production of *Lord Pengo* alone. Mostly the sentiments were thanking her for her thoughtfulnesses one way or another. She was a very thoughtful person, but in a very private way.

I was privileged to read her own copy of *Lord Pengo*'s printed souvenir brochure, complete with pictures of the cast, etc. One of her cohorts signed his photo, "You have changed my life." Henry Danielle wrote, "Such memories of soap and cheese." She was often a nut about soap (especially wonderfully scented and beautifully produced soaps), and she was just as interested in good cheese—fine cheese in true Wisconsin fashion.

It occurred to me you might like to know what the competition was like on Broadway in 1962 at the very time *Lord Pengo* was playing. Contemporary with Agnes, Boyer, and their cast that season were: Joseph Cotten in *Calculated Risk*, Anthony Quinn in *Tchin Tchin*, Jason Robards, Jr., in *A Thousand Clowns*, Kathryn Grayson in *Camelot*, Robert Morse, Rudy Valee in *How to Succeed in Business without Really Trying*, Emlyn Williams in *A Man for All Seasons*, Sid Caesar in *Little Me*, Barbara Bel Geddes in *Mary, Mary*, Robert Ryan in *Mr. President*, plus *Sound of Music, Oliver, Never Too Late, Who's Afraid of Virginia Woolf?*

Her biographical sketch in the brochure for *Lord Pengo* said: "Toured more than any other actress living or dead. Once rode a circus elephant, played little Eva on a Mississippi riverboat, and scared the whey out of a nation with her performance of the doomed woman on the radio production of *Sorry, Wrong Number.*"

When interviewed backstage once, she told me she thinks of theater as a place of instructive entertainment where you can sit and learn to laugh or cry. "I'm not going to ever contribute to delinquency in my roles, either adult or juvenile delinquency. I think too much of the public." This was the zeal Joseph Cotten mentioned and the evangelical professional fervor Agnes exemplified.

Somehow, with movies, television, and all sorts of assignments, Agnes managed to sandwich in the musical comedy *High Spirits* in the twenty-fourth season of Dallas Summer Musical Theater, 1965. It was produced by Tom Hughes and directed by John Bishop. Based on Noel Coward's *Blithe Spirit*, the music, lyrics, and book were by Hugh Martin and Timothy Gray. Agnes played the part of Madame Arcati, who held a seance for a member of the cast. Michael Evans and Iva Withers were in the cast. In the biography of Agnes in the brochure of the musical comedy, they credit her with *Don Juan in Hell* appearances in Dallas with the First Drama Quartette and three personal appearances of her readings. (More of this in the next chapter.)

Even some of Miss Moorehead's most ardent fans in movies and television have little idea of her versatility on the boards, including several musical comedies. The very last vehicle she appeared in was *Gigi*. About the mid-sixties she also appeared with Ginger Rogers, Leif Erickson, and Maggie Hayes in *Pink Jungle*. It was produced by her long-time friend and mentor, Paul Gregory. Music and lyrics were by Vernon Duke, and direction was by Joseph Anthony.

When she would be touring, thoughtful people were constantly writing for Agnes to come to the country for lunch, dinner, or just plain rest, since touring is so hard, even for the stars. Generals, statesmen, school presidents, financiers, industrialists, every imaginable person wrote to help her escape the dreary routine of hotels and drearier food, often eaten on the run or hurriedly backstage between rehearsals or between matinee and evening performances.

Since she was so thoughtful, especially with hospitalized veterans, it is no wonder that a Fort Dix, New Jersey, writer would say that this past-middle-age woman "got a warmer reception than Miss New Jersey and was the biggest hit as long as anyone could remember."

Keep in mind that while touring, in addition to constant travel plans, packing, unpacking, and personal needs, there were unlimited requests for every imaginable kind of personal appearance.

In 1972, while in Chicago with the second go-round for *Don Juan in Hell* (nearly twenty years after the First Quartette), there were radio interviews, newspaper interviews, magazine interviews, and television interviews—such as *Kup's Show* (Irv Kupcinet), and Essee Kupcinet persuaded Agnes to appear at the Jefferson Awards Dinner, Israel's twenty-fifth birthday, and National Artists' Committee. It boggles the mind that this rather frail woman—who was neither stout nor tall—this constant trouper, the "Queen of the Road," still found time for innumerable requests in her already very busy schedule. Small wonder she longed for the farm in southeastern Ohio. Small wonder she was eagerly awaiting the finish of each tour so she could rest and regroup—refine her sensitive spiritual qualities.

Agnes nearly didn't return to the second go-round of *Don Juan in Hell*. But she said motion pictures are mostly so tawdry (not all of them), so devoid of the real sense of life, she decided to go out again with it.

This time, John Houseman directed it. He gave all sorts of credit to Agnes' help and suggestions, based on her original tour twenty years earlier. This time the cast was: Don Juan: Ricardo Montalban; Satan: Edward Mulhare; the Commander: Paul Henried; and Dona Ana: Agnes Moorehead.

They opened in Boston for two weeks in October 1972. Then to Washington for three weeks. Next Cincinnati for one week. December found them in Philadelphia, Pittsburg, and Wilmington, Delaware; Toronto for the New Year and two weeks afterward; New York for four weeks—mid-January to mid-February.

Mary Astor wrote in her book *Mary Astor: A Life on Film* (Dell Books, 1967): "There was a road company being formed for *Don Juan in Hell*, a section of Shaw's *Man and Superman*. Agnes Moorehead, Charles Laughton, and Charles Boyer had been enormously successful in a very interesting theatrical innovation. It was presented without scenery by four players who carried large, impressive, leather-bound manuscripts onto the stage, opened them on lecterns, and sat or stood and *apparently* read the play to the audience. It wasn't read, it was memorized and played, the 'readers' gradually becoming the characters in the play.

"The company assembled in a small, attractive playhouse-cum-workshop above Santa Monica Boulevard for rehearsals. Kurt Kasznar, Ricardo Montalban, Reginald Denny, and I, and Agnes Moorehead as our director.

"Here there was none of the depressing 'You're lookin' fine, sweetie!' None of that 'dear old girl' crap. Here we concentrated on Shaw and his words and his thinking. Agnes, besides being an excellent actress, is a fine director and was most generous with her own experience in the show. (This was not a case of following a personal success by another actress. For Agnes gave me all sorts of little goodies which she had found and worked when she originated the show. I wasn't working blind.)"

Since she was on tour with *Gigi* the following year, she had to miss her coveted Christmas party, which always coincided with her birthday, two years in a row—1972 and 1973. This was to mean she would never preside at one again.

Here were some of the tabloid's comments on the second go-round of *Don Juan in Hell* as found in Agnes' theatrical souvenirs: "Talk in a Hot Spot." "Going to Hell Demands Cool Head." "Don Juan is Theater of the Intellect." "Shaw's Talkathon in Good Hands." "Heavenly Presentation of Shaw's Devilish Wit." "Superb Performances Bring Don Juan to Life." One reviewer wrote: "Miss Moorehead never having seemed really young, she will never truly grow old. She is one of our most skillful stage technicians."

Ken Mayer, Boston *Herald Traveler* (October 26, 1972) said: "Agnes Moorehead is the heir apparent to the throne vacated by the great Ethel Barrymore. Great is too weak a word to describe her."

Faithful Cesar Romero sent her flowers and an opening-night telegram, "Break a leg. I'll be talking to you."

Joseph Cotten reminded us she was ever crusading for better acting, better vehicles, and more beauty, more gentility, and, above all, more appeal to the spirit in the theater.

One of the last things she told me on the phone went something like this: "I hope family life, good solid family life, comes back. It means so much to the world. It means so much to the children. I feel sad for some of these youngsters. There's not a wholesome laugh of life in them. There's nothing like learning to laugh. They're kind of bent. They're old before their time. They're old at seventeen. And when it comes to marriage—they're really babes in the woods." I often played the devil's advocate in these discussions by pointing out how modern families contribute to the so-called juvenile delinquency by being torn apart constantly with false priorities.

Once again, I can hear her say so eloquently and poignantly,

"I don't want to drag audiences into the gutter and push them into the mud. I want the theater to be spiritual uplift even while entertaining. It should be glorious, too."

8
Fabulous Redhead

With the inspiration of Charles Laughton and the production know-how of Paul Gregory, Agnes was literally pushed into going on the road with her famous One Nighters. She changed the material to suit the audiences regionally, daytime or nighttime, whether all student, all adult, or mixed. Once she was encouraged to step forth as only she could have done, who knows how many more miles of touring she racked up to make her undisputed Queen of the Road? It must have been hundreds of thousands of miles, when one includes her overseas One Nighters, too.

She worked the readings from 1954 to 1970, although once she was committed to *Bewitched*, she had neither time nor the energy to perform as much in what became her favorite media.

Hardy Price, formerly of Texas and now of Phoenix, recalls her reading from the telephone directory on one occasion. Her voice, her diction, and dramatics held him enthralled even with such lowbrow reading. Mostly she read selections from James Thurber, Ring Lardner, Rupert Brooks, de Maupassant, Marcel Proust, the Bible, *Don Juan in Hell*, and, on request, *Sorry, Wrong Number*.

As time passed, she added new material and dropped former favorites. Edna St. Vincent Millay, Robert Frost, George Bernard Shaw, and particulars like *Hush, Hush, Sweet Charlotte* and "Ballad of the Harp Weaver."

She never tired of doing Thurber material. Some of his books are prominent parts of her personal library. She liked to recall that she used to lunch in a corner of the Algonquin Hotel with James Thurber. "I asked to use some of his material," she said. "Do you know what he said? 'You and Lionel Barrymore gave me so much pleasure that you can use anything of mine. Free.' The last time I saw him he was blind. When I neared his table, he said, 'I'd know that voice anywhere, Agnes Moorehead. And I want to thank you because I sold more books just because of your popular readings.' Wasn't that sweet of him?"

Repeatedly, whenever she was asked if someone should go into acting, she would give them her grande dame look and say, "Only if you have courage, strength, and patience. And always remember, no matter how successful you become, if you do not keep working at it, you can soon fall by the wayside."

When she was touring, she had a pat philosophy to give each interviewer. It went something like this: "An actor is like a wandering minstrel and thus must sell his talent to the whole country. Touring is an eye-opener because the culture is not just in New York City and the West Coast. There are marvelous audiences all over our great country. [No wonder she loved America so much.] I always say you haven't played an audience until you've played Stillwater, Oklahoma."

One reviewer in her souvenirs, speaking of her One Nighters, said : "Miss Moorehead demonstrated the sometimes forgotten truth that people, not gimmicks, make the theater."

Another of her favorite philosophies that she shared over and over again was about actors and actresses staying aloof. "The reason some actors tend to socialize with their own is not snobbism but merely a case of protecting themselves. My profession is sacred to me. I'm happy when people like a performance but I can't help it when they don't. This is a responsibility I have to shoulder. Some kind of protection from the public at times is absolutely necessary. Because we give and give and give, one must keep something for oneself. It is imperative one doesn't exhaust himself forever in private life, too. I believe the artist should be kept separated somewhat to maintain glamor and a kind of mystery. Otherwise we'd be just like three meals a day, and that can be pretty dull."

It would be impossible to list the many places Agnes did her crowd-pleasing one-woman show. I came across a reference to her appearing at Odessa College in Texas in 1965.

Pat Stout, the executive secretary of the Scottsdale, Arizona, Dinner Club, wrote me that Agnes had appeared there October 23, 1969. I recall the evening vividly. Mrs. Stout added to my memories by mentioning that Agnes refused to eat the customary dinner for speaking guests. Instead she paced up and down, up and down, in a secluded passageway at Mountain Shadows Resort. When they were ready for her, she walked quickly to the podium and launched into an unforgettable series of readings.

It was not until after the presentation that Agnes would even dream of eating. Before she sat down to eat, I mentioned to her that our children had helped to elect her the favorite actress of their school. *Bewitched* was mostly responsible, of course.

I came across another mention in her files of appearing at the Cherry County Playhouse, Traverse City, Michigan, that same year of 1969. What was unusual was she actually appeared there *all week* in a series of readings only. The other weeks starred: Anne Jeffrys in *Anniversary Waltz*, Tom Kennedy in *There's a Girl in My Soup*, and Maureen O'Sullivan in *Butterflies Are Free*.

Of all the references to Moorehead's One Nighters, I liked the following from an old San Diego Evening *Tribune*. It was done by Karen Gustafson, but had no date. She headlined her column: "Agnes Moorehead Turns Old Into New."

A great act can make a familiar old story sound like a new one. That's what Agnes Moorehead does [with her 'Fabulous Redhead' reading].

She gives the Biblical story of the Flood, heard so many times before, or, Robert Frost's "Stopping By The Woods" and makes everyone hear them in a new way. What was witnessed last night was one of the country's few great ladies of the Theater at work. She brought us out laughing with household hints of the fourteenth, sixteenth and nineteenth centuries. Her stage manner, movement, improved by generations of actresses is unforgettable. The sweeping gesture, the casual pacing of a Greek chorus. I thought her rendition of George Bernard Shaw's *Don Juan in Hell* was outstanding. It was a natural for an actress of her stature. A real crowd pleaser was her telling of a fictitious cousin, Daphne, retelling her version of Moses in the bullrushes. Either way, as grande dame or crowd pleaser, the audience loved her. After all, she'd earned over many years the right to that love.

9
Madame Mauve

Violet, purple, lavender, mauve, lilac — her favorite color or shade. Freddie and Polly each sent her birthday cards on mauve stationery addressed to "Madame Mauve." She had their complete wardrobes done in what she liked to call "Moorehead Mauve." These dresses included their morning dresses and pinafores.

Anything violet or purple mauvish won her instant adulation and praise. Her purple Thunderbird is still parked in the back driveway. She loved Parma violets. She had a spot of the color somewhere in every room at both the house and the farm.

If she liked violets, there was never anything shrinking about her. With her red hair and part-Irish ancestry, she was renowned for her fiery wit. She always looked taller than her actual height of about five foot three. When one first met her, there was a charming combination of the reserve of a private person and yet somewhat expansive personality. She was bewitching.

Agnes loved animals. The French poodles have already been noted. Her favorite was an old English bull terrier named Cluny. She kept in one of her more intimate files a clipping about bull terriers. It said of her favorite dog: "Keen intelligence, good judgment, delightful sense of humor, sincere craving for human affection. Seldom barks or is noisy. Has legendary strength and tenacity. Doesn't require much exercise and short harsh coat is easily maintained." Every one of these traits appealed to her. Cluny seems to miss the mistress of the house, whereas the French poodles have adjusted to her absence.

Returning to Christmas cards and parties for a moment, I should mention that the Edward Robinsons, the Edgar Bergens, and the Basil Rathbones annually invited her to their Christmas feasts. David and Jennifer Selznick always replied by telegram if they were unable to attend her Christmas party.

Cesar Romero said: "The annual party was not just for entertainment people. Besides movie, television, radio, stage, and recording stars, she always invited politicians, artists, industrialists, writers, producers, directors, business tycoons, and very often, just plain folks."

Agnes liked to describe her home as a Mediterranean villa but Venetian in character. In addition to drapes, chandeliers with odd-shaped shells protruding from the ends, antiques and knights' masks, which only a compulsive collector could amass, she liked to call her general decor a "mass of clean clutter."

There is an interesting story of how she obtained the seashell chandeliers. It was her intent to try to mask the beamed ceilings that were part of the late Sigmund Romberg's home.

Villa Agnese is in the same block as the homes of Polly Bergen and Lucille Ball. Oscar Levant and Ira Gershwin, and Jack Benny also lived nearby. Jimmy Stewart and Rosemary

Clooney still do. I kidded her once, "I'd sure like to have a block party here in your block."

Just as Sunday was usually her disciplined day of rest and renewal of spirit and mind, Saturday was usually shopping day, errand day, and general catch-up day. She painted. She liked to play the piano. She liked to putter around. I asked Polly Garland if it was true that she even liked to rake leaves.

Polly Garland told me: "Oh, yes. She liked to putter with the broom. She even used to climb a very high ladder to wash the windows up there [pointing] at what you call the clerestory. She must have inherited the trait of cleanliness, because although it was clutter, it was always clean clutter."

Her stern faith would also appear in the cleanliness trait inasmuch as there is the saying "Cleanliness is next to Godliness." On the topic of personal cleanliness, she used to admit to being both a shower and a bath person. She once dubbed her kingsize bed "Moorehouse Stadium."

Throughout her home, as at the farm, there is a constant reminder of her fondness for animals. There are two large ceramic lions at either side of the massive ancient front door. Her long-time friend, Cesar Romero, is very fond of elephants. He has a fascinating collection of them, including a favorite given to him by Agnes. Among her kept telegrams is one from Romero that mentions elephants. I've already mentioned the two tile ones she has in her rumpus room.

With her affection for things purple and mauve, it could be said that she was born to the purple, for her nobility of heritage was always precious to her. She came from a long line of prelates who brought esteem to the cloth. Over and over again she was to mention with gracefulness her religious faith. We discussed this many times. In practically every interview she ever gave anyone, she would mention her faith. For example, she told me: "The religion of my parents and of the generation before no longer prevails in a world of cold wars and atomic explosions. That may be enough for some persons, but I find I can't accept such thinking. I read the Bible first thing each morning and the last thing each night."

What prompted her to testify so much about her faith? She was proud of her heritage and of her beliefs. She often said, "I believe in the old-fashioned notions about the efficacy of prayer." But what caused her to *always* mention her Presbyterian minister father?

Was it because of the vinegary women she often portrayed? Was it fear that others might think she was as bewitched as many of the unladylike characters she portrayed? Surely these women were anything but the very private person Agnes was— anything but the ladylike woman with purely private cherished beliefs and a personal philosophy of her craft and the will and wit to practice what she believed. Her Americanism could be aroused with the slightest criticism of a president (any president), of her beloved country, of our American way.

One cannot help wondering if the deep thrust of her faith and fundamentalist religion may have cost her far more deeply than she may have been privately aware of. That she was wont to "keep her counsel" as Mary of old only solidified her being a very private person.

She often reiterated, "My life has been ruled by my beliefs."

Her philosophy was never limited to her religious faith. Her belief in her craftsmanship was also paramount. Though a private person, she was a many-faceted person. Just as there was a little of Agnes in every character she played, there were also different dispositions.

If you were to meet her at a late supper party, she might seem demure, beguiling, and, as one person put it, "a favorite aunt." She could also be sharp, testy, snappy. If anyone remarked about this, she'd rejoin: "I'm a redhead and Scotch-Irish. I admire people with drive and ambition." And when she put on her regal, glamorous movie bit, look out. There has never been anyone quite like her.

Agnes really believed there was too much mediocrity in the films and on the stage. She often repeated she was not interested in feeding people tawdriness, chaos, and confusion.

There was entirely too much use of foul language. Words were important in her credo. She invariably spoke of the necessity of reverence for words.

As for method acting, she said: "No such thing as *a* method. You can't stereotype talent. You can train what you have, though. It is difficult for young actors today, where there is so little time for beauty and true romance."

She liked to rhetorically ask, "How does one fit art into the atomic age?" This was constantly on her mind from *Sputnik* onward. "The arts are being crowded out when they should be companions instead of rivals." Then she would lament about the dearth of mysticism. (More on that later.) Then she would return to art, in that quicker-than-lightning mind of hers, saying, "Where is the corner from which all art is born? Much of it comes from the home, the family. Alas, children are not taught respect and reverence as they once were. Hence very little attention to creative art and creative living, let alone any attention to the Creator of it all."

Persons who knew her at all always caught something of her magic of humor, in addition to the magic of her intellect, philosophy, and charm. There are many humorous cards sprinkled throughout her mementoes. One said "Fear not, some day your SHIP will come in and you'll be waiting at the railroad depot."

Lucille Ball, her Scrabble partner, once sent her a card from Hawaii:

Dear Agnes—Scrabblehead,
We are sitting here on Diamond *Head*—soon *head*ing for home. Will beat card home even though I'm giving it a *head* start.
(1967)   Lucy

Agnes not only received thousands of fan letters, cards, wires, notes, and every possible means of communication but sent out thousands. She took time to write managers of hotels, motels, inns. They in turn would compliment her for her thoughtfulness, which was way beyond necessity or duty. What always impressed me was that she took time. The little more and how much it is (the little less and how it whiles away).

A postcard from a fan in 1962 said:

Dear Miss Moorehead:
These humble words are sincere.
Like a tree has roots, you are a root of the Theater.
Like the Lion is the King of the Jungle, you are a Queen of the Stage.
Like Rodin was a master in his field, you are a master in yours.
What Sara Bernhardt meant to others of her time
This is what you are and mean to me.
                    Most sincerely
                    (unsigned)

If this were from a drama student, there are hundreds of records of persons telling her how thankful they were for her visit to their drama class—whether it was in a private school, public school, college, or university. Not once did she ever mention or complain of the heavy extra burden of time, effort, and physical, mental, and nervous power carried to meet these additional strains on her being.

Another card bore this little idea:

A ctive
G enerous
N ice
E xciting
S tar

Every motion picture star, television and stage personality must receive requests from every kind of person for just about every conceivable purpose. Agnes was no different. Letters poured in asking for her favorite recipe, rules for success, pets' names ad infinitum. One person actually sent her a list of twenty questions relating to a former co-star. There were scores of requests regarding term papers, theses, and dissertations. That she must have favored many of these requests is testimony to volumes of scrapbooks filled with letters of appreciation and gratitude for favors extended. When one realizes how few ever show courtesy or thankfulness and gratitude, it shows all the more how fantastic her answers and helpfulness must have truly been.

She must have liked languages. There is evidence that she taught herself French. She had several other language books (Greek, Italian, Spanish). She kept several language newspapers, including those of the above mentioned plus Israeli and Arabic. It seems likely that she would learn enough of each to "get by on" in her travels.

Her fan mail came from the remotest as well as the exotic countries: Iceland, Ireland, Yugoslavia, Sweden, Haiti, Brazil, Indonesia, Philippines, and Colombia, just to mention a few.

My favorite card was an eight by ten colored card from Switzerland from Paulette Goddard (Mrs. Erich Remarque).

I can testify to her being a sparkling conversationalist and among the best-read persons I've ever known, including Clare Booth Luce and the late Pearl S. Buck. It's always nice to hear it repeated by other admirers.

Every successful person is apt to get on the appeals lists. Agnes received appeals from every conceivable charity. On the same page that there was a thank-you note for speaking to a gospel mission in downtown New York, there was a letter from a friend using such words as: clerisy, solecisms, malaprops, sycophancy. What a woman!

On one of the tables in the rumpus room were the following autographed photos: from Lucy Ball—"For Aggie—my favorite Actress. My pleasure to know such a beautiful lady. s. Gary & his favorite wife, Lucy." From Mickey Rooney—"To Agnes—one of the real people in the business. I hope we will work more together. s. Mickey." From Henry Fonda—"For Aggie—with all my love. s. Hank." From Marcel Marceau— "To Agnes—with admiration and devotion. s. Marcel." From Jerry Lewis—"For a great lady, Agnes—Thank you for giving my film the touch of class it has. Always. s. Jerry."

10
Television

Bewitched was launched in 1963. At first Agnes treated it as just another vehicle. She was dumbfounded that it became so popular. Still, because of her beliefs about clean entertainment, she was not really surprised. Agnes told me on several occasions that she liked the part of Endora because as she got into it, she realized it turned order out of chaos.

Another time she said, "I believe a theme like *Bewitched* is a wholesome reversal of the bunk and trend toward sordidness." Her strong feelings about the philosophy of her craftsmanship were never more evident than in the part of Endora. She said, "The magic an actor has should be used to release the human heart. You can go just so far with this neurotic stuff. The human spirit needs something else."

Continuing about her favorite role as Endora, she said, "You should never know what she's going to do. The stranger the spot she is occupying, the better. That's what is marvelous about playing comedy, playing for the unexpected. It's distorted from reality, and therefore the happening becomes a surprise. After all, nothing is as dull as constant reality."

When interviewers appeared amazed at what a private person Agnes was, she would toss it off with that verve of hers, "I've never wanted to be a personality. I've always tried to be completely different in my characterizations."

It was to be expected that several attempts at copies of *Bewitched* sprang into being, that is, along the line of the supernatural. When asked if she minded others copying their very successful series, Agnes said, "Just remember the original always wears better than the copy. Besides, we already have our audience."

Hal Humphrey in the Los Angeles *Times* [7-23-65] said, "The reason Agnes Moorehead always wears so well is because she is an original."

People often thought Agnes was English because of her nearly perfect diction. She remarked: "I've noticed that English actresses nearly always have good diction, but I supposed it was because they learn acting in the theater instead of via movies, television, and the like."

As a matter of fact, there was a great deal of the British Isles in her family background. She was proud that her paternal grandfather was from Edinburgh and that her paternal grandmother was from London. Her maternal grandmother was from Dublin and her maternal grandfather was from Wales.

The first review I could find of her part in *Bewitched* was by Don Freeman. There was no date or name of the paper on the review clipped out. Mr. Freeman said: "Agnes Moorehead is, as always, a tower of eminence." The producers were later to write in more and more parts for her as time went on.

Agnes was always charmed to have children come up to her and meekly say, "Aren't you gonna disappear?"

Since she had such a fondness for lavender or mauve, it was no surprise that her dressing room for *Bewitched* was done in lavender.

I thought it was Biblically fitting that Agnes played the part of Endora, since I suppose the name was based on the witch of Endor, so famous in the Old Testament. It would have pleased her to play the part of such a witch so many centuries after Bible times.

My first remembrance of her was that she cast a spell

Endora from *Bewitched*, with Elizabeth Montgomery.

offstage as well as on, off camera as well as on. The Titian hair, the blue eyes, and the voice that was unforgettable. She was shorter than I had imagined.

At first I was startled by her deadpan face. As many came to realize, one could begin to measure her real intent by her voice. Her mood was usually indicated by her voice. When she really wanted to confuse someone, she did it with those bewitching eyes.

In addition to the scores of movie films and the scores of *Bewitched* episodes, Agnes also appeared in over one hundred television productions. Add to these tremendous achievements the hundreds of radio shows, hundreds of personal appearances, and endless reading appearances plus recording and voice-overs, one's mind is boggled by her prodigious feats. Way back when she was given the New York Film Critic's Award for her performance in *The Magnificent Ambersons*, it was said that she was a scholar and a protean artist. The ensuing years only attest to the achievements of this great lady.

Some of her television shows were: *Ballad of Andy Crocker*, with Jimmy Dean, Lee Majors, Pat Hingle; *Barefoot in the Park*, a pilot for ABC; *Wagon Train*; *Playhouse 90*; Shirley Temple's Theater productions of *Rapunzel* and *Land of Oz*; *The Rebel*; *Studio One*; *Twilight Zone*; *The Rifleman*; Rex Harrison's Anthology: *Epicac* by Kurt Vonnegut, *Kiss Me Again, Stranger* by Daphne Du Maurier; *The Fortunate Painter*, with Lorne Green, Jess Walton, written by Somerset Maugham.

A Walt Disney show with Burgess Meredith [10-31-71].

One of her last, if not the last, was *Dr. Frankenstein* in 1973.

The Tempest with the late Van Heflin in 1967 (she received much mail for this).

Alice Through the Looking Glass, [11-6-66] reputed to be the most expensive set since Mary Martin's celebrated *Peter Pan* — over half a million dollars. This was made with Jimmy Durante, Nanette Fabray, Ricardo Montalban, and Jack Palance, plus some others.

She appeared in countless telethons for every conceivable

type of charity. Agnes was the guest on most panel talk shows, including those of Steve Allen, Joey Bishop, Johnny Carson, Mike Douglas, Irv Kupinet. Hollywood Palace claimed her, too.

For several years before her death, Agnes' agent was Jim Jacobsen of International Famous Agency. He told me: "Do you see that Emmy nomination on the wall? Agnes insisted I have it. Not many persons would do that. From all the stars I've known, she was a Super Lady. I don't know how else to describe her." He went on, "She was client, friend, an absolute perfectionist. We worked together six years. That's a long time in this business.

"The first time I attended one of her annual Christmas parties, I supposed it would be informal and arrived in sweater and slacks. Agnes pointed out to me one of the top stars who was in a tuxedo. It wasn't a putdown, she just wanted me to subtly know she hoped I'd dress more appropriately in the future. So, came the next year, she was plainly petrified that *her* agent might turn up informal again. So for weeks she reminded me, 'Please, please at least wear black pinstripes and try to look like *my* agent should look.' I obliged her, of course. She was too great a lady to do otherwise.

"Negotiating contracts are always a headache, especially the little details. It's the little details that sometimes knock you out! Well, we called one year the 'Year of the Kleenex Clause.' You know Agnes, she was always running out of them. Her intense makeup for the part of Endora was murder on Kleenex. With all the joking about it, she was still very adamant that—*one*, there always was to be an adequate supply; *two*, they must be of particular size; *three*, you know her passion for purple—they must be a particular color; and *four*, above all, they had to be a particular brand. Well, we finally came to terms, but it was some year." The little more and how much it is!

11
Awardography

If the film-listing chapter is entitled "Filmography" then perhaps this chapter is aptly entitled "Awardography."

MOVIES:

Oscar — Certificate for Nomination for Award: Agnes Moorehead nominated for Academy Award of Merit, supporting actress in *Hush, Hush, Sweet Charlotte*, December 31, 1964.

The Film Daily: Filmdom's Famous Fibes of 1954. Agnes Moorehead, whose creative contributions to the screen's progress were foremost in 1954. December 27, 1954. (This year included *Magnificent Obsession*.)

Motion Picture Relief Fund Testimonial: "Recognition to Agnes Moorehead for unselfish services you contributed on behalf of your Motion Picture Relief Fund, May 31, 1943."

Box Office Blue Ribbon Awards: "Best Picture of the Month"
September, 1944, to Agnes Moorehead in *The Seventh Cross* (MGM) with Spencer Tracy.
December, 1944, to Agnes Moorehead in *Mrs. Parkington* (MGM) with Greer Garson, Walter Pidgeon.
October, 1945, to Agnes Moorehead in *Our Vines Have Tender Grapes* (MGM) with Edward G. Robinson.
November, 1948, to Agnes Moorehead in *Johnny Belinda* (Warner Bros.) with Jane Wyman.
July, 1949, to Agnes Moorehead in *The Stratton Story* (MGM) with James Stewart.
July, 1960, to Agnes Moorehead in *Pollyanna* (Buena Vista) with Jane Wyman, Karl Malden.
April, 1966, to Agnes Moorehead in *The Singing Nun* (MGM) with Debbie Reynolds.

Motion Picture Exhibitor International Laurel Award:
Agnes Moorehead Top 5 Supporting Performance 1965
Agnes Moorehead Top 5 Supporting Role 1966
Also 1951, 1952.
Also 1954, 1955.
Also 1956, 1957, 1958.

Hollywood Foreign Press Association: Golden Globe Award to
Agnes Moorehead as Best Supporting Actress in 1964 in *Hush,
Hush, Sweet Charlotte.*

New York Film Critics: Best performance by an actress in
1942—to Agnes Moorehead in *The Magnificent Ambersons.*

TELEVISION:

National Academy of Television Arts and Sciences: Certificate
of nomination to Agnes Moorehead for the outstanding performance by an actress in supporting role in a comedy for her
role in *Bewitched*, 1965-1966. Repeat 1966-1967, 1967-1968,
1968-1969.
To Agnes Moorehead for "Night of the Vicious Valentine" on
Wild, Wild West, February 10, 1967, (received this and *Bewitched* nomination same year. Won Emmy for this one.)

1964 T.V. and Radio Mirror: Editor's Award to Agnes Moorehead for tragic and comic roles on television and radio.

Los Angeles Metropolitan District, California Federation of
Women's Clubs' Tenth Anniversary Convention awarded
Agnes Moorehead the television award for her performance in
Bewitched, 1966.

RADIO:

Pacific Pioneer Broadcasters: Pioneer in Broadcasting Industry
Award to Agnes Moorehead.

Golden Mike Award: Best performance in suspense radio in
1953 to Agnes Moorehead in *Sorry, Wrong Number.*

Distinguished Achievement Award: 1945-1946 to Agnes Moorehead for distinguished achievement during the radio season 1945-1946 as outstanding dramatic performer in *Sorry, Wrong Number*.

RARE HONORS:

B'Nai B'rith's Human Relations Award: to Agnes Moorehead, "whose personal and dedicated commitment to enhancing individual dignity and respect, promoting better intergroup understanding, and securing equal rights and opportunities for all, have strengthened and enriched America's democratic heritage," Anti-Defamation League of B'Nai B'rith, December 4, 1966.

The U. S. Commander, Berlin: (Her Americanism beliefs made her *so* proud of this one!) Agnes Moorehead, having dwelt east of the Elbe and behind the Iron Curtain, having joined the Berlin garrison in the forefront of free world resistance to Communism and having indicated unyielding support for the cause of freedom in this divided city, is in recognition from this day forth hereby designated "A Guardian of Berlin's Freedom," May 4, 1968 (while reviewing GI plays tour).

"The Play's the Thing" "Because Agnes Moorehead generously gave of her time and herself, for the purpose of providing a fund with which to buy theater tickets for visitors from foreign countries, the Minnesota International Center has been able to host 107 persons from abroad at theatrical productions at the University of Minnesota, the Tyrone Guthrie Theater, Metropolitan Opera, The Stagecoach Playhouse, Theater in the Round, St. Paul Theater and other amateur theaters in metropolitan area.

"The names of the visitors who have enjoyed good theater, because of the A. M. Fund are listed below. We are pleased to present Agnes Moorehead with this *SCROLL* as a token of deep appreciation of the visitors and the Minnesota International Center." There followed names from these countries:

84

Africa: Angola, Chad, Egypt, Ghana, Malagasy, Mozambique, Tanganyika, Union of South Africa, Upper Volta, Nigeria.

Middle East: Iraq, Israel, Turkey.

Latin America: Chile, Colombia, Dominican Republic, French Guiana, Haiti, Jamaica, Mexico, Nicaragua, Venezuela.

Europe: England, Germany, Greece, Italy, Norway, Poland, Spain, Netherlands, Sweden, Yugoslavia, Iceland, Faroe Islands.

Asia: Federation of Malaya, India, Pakistan, Philippines, Japan, Korea, Thailand, Vietnam.

Australia and New Zealand.

COLLEGES:

Certificates from Glacier College, Kalispell, Montana, November 1, 1965; Nazareth College Alumni, October 10, 1964; Muskingum College, New Concord, Ohio, 1965; Alpha Psi Omega, dramatic fraternity, April 25, 1966, to Agnes Moorehead for meritorious participation in college dramatics; Monmouth College, Illinois, honorary degree of doctor of fine arts, April 26, 1959; Muskingum College, honorary degree, doctor of literature, June 9, 1947.

Bradley University
Peoria, Illinois
May 31, 1959
from Dean Olive B. White:

Mr. President:

The lady whom I have the honor to present to you is a brilliant actress and teacher. Born in Boston, she was brought as a child to the Middle West where she received her schooling. She is a graduate of Muskingum College, Ohio, and won her Master's degree in English and Speech at the University of Wisconsin.

The spell of the theater enticed her, however, from the

classroom and the amateur theater to New York, the American Academy of Dramatic Arts, and fairer fortune on stage, radio and T.V. than rewards many a neophyte in that stern art. With Orson Welles and Joseph Cotten, she collaborated in founding the Mercury Theater. Thence she went to Hollywood and the triumphs of *Citizen Kane, The Magnificent Ambersons, Mrs. Parkington, Johnny Belinda, Magnificent Obsession, Jeanne Eagels, The Tempest* — to name but a few of the 48 films (as of 1959) to which her talent has brought her distinction. Four times she has been nominated for Academy Awards and she has won other prized citations.

Neither New York or Hollywood has monopolized her gifts, however, for she has proved herself a trouper in the brave old tradition, twice in this very fieldhouse, starring in stellar company she has given us the memorable theater experience of *Don Juan in Hell* and *The Rivalry*.

She is a teacher still, and a glad one in her direction of private drama classes and in her seminar at U.S.C.

It's a privilege, Mr. President, to present for the degree of Doctor of Fine Arts the distinguished dramatic artist, Agnes Moorehead.

OTHER AWARDS:

First Writer's Award: to Agnes Moorehead for participation in *Tomorrow the World* (a Lester Cowan Production), January 30, 1945.

There are a host of awards too numerous to mention for participating in every manner of charity and helpfulness you can imagine. For example:

The city of Los Angeles designated her ambassador at large, April 12, 1967.

The city of Paducah, Kentucky made her Duchess of Paducah, June 29, 1961.

The State of Louisiana appointed her Honorary Brigadier

General on staff of Governor John McKeithen, June 3, 1964. *San Francisco Jaycees* honored her. *The Los Angeles Philharmonic, California Institute of Technology,* even *George Gershwin Junior High,* cited her for humane work on behalf of the youth of America. She was cited numerous times during World War II for services to war funds, etc.

Her contributions to Jewish Welfare both here and in Israel were numerous, and her constant interest in Jewish cultural affairs included Israel Festival of Music, which cited her at a Waldorf Astoria banquet.

Citations, certificates, trophies, and awards lined every bit of the four walls and shelves of her private office beyond the rumpus room. It was characteristic of this very private person to not parade these hundreds of awards where even visitors could ever see them. Instead, she kept them in the intimacy of her private office.

12
Multi-Dimensional Life

One of the banes but also blessings of an entertainer's life has to be the interminable list of invitations. Here is just a sampling of the persons who wanted Agnes at some function or other: Rod McKuen, Ross Hunter, John Houseman, Walt Disney, Virginia Graham, Marcel Marceau, Glenn Ford, Ivy Baker Priest, Jimmy Durante, the Marriotts, L. A. Mayor Sam Yorty, President and Mrs. Nixon, Mervyn LeRoy, Rosalind Russell, Bob and Delores Hope, Dan Duryea, Mrs. Nat King Cole, Joan Crawford, Sharman Douglas, Jimmy and Gloria Stewart.

Mr. and Mrs. Quincy Jones invited her to a "two-fisted" fashion show at which Mohammed Ali would appear. The Edward G. Robinsons asked her to view their art treasures for Recording for the Blind. The Arthur Hays Sulzbergers and Arthur Ochs Sulzbergers asked her to meet with the Board of Directors of Associated Press (April 18, 1965). She was invited to meet Princess Margaret and the Earl of Snowden (November, 1965). That Christmastide the Sinatra children invited her to their party at the Beverly Wilshire (December 12, 1965).

When she attended the opening of Montreal Expo on behalf of Screen Gems, the producers of *Bewitched*, she was described as looking regal. One description was, "She looked like an empress without a country, clad in royal purple trimmed in chinchilla."

Doris Warner Vidor invited her to a special meeting of Vietnam USO work at the San Souci Room of the Beverly Wilshire (November 7, 1965) with Raymond Burr and the under secretary of the Air Force. Ms. Vidor said she was flying out from New York just for the meeting. Incidentally, there is frequent use of Western Union messages for these kinds of invitations.

There is much evidence that Agnes took time to write many officers and servicemen in Vietnam, to judge from letters received from them.

One airman from George Air Force Base thanked her for holding the men spellbound when she appeared there to read from Shakespeare and the Bible. It was always her utmost best for God and country.

Several times we had little coincidences in our mutual lifetimes. The most recent for me was to note that she was invited to read from Shakespeare at the Hollywood Bowl on the 400th Anniversary of the Bard of Avon. The date: July 11, 1964. That was exactly ten years to the day that I began research of her lengthy career.

A little note was saved from her Shakespeare readings at Trenton, New Jersey (March, 1965). It said: "Expected excellence in your readings and poised presence, but was totally unprepared for the beauty and grace which will long adorn my memory."

The Hon. James Roosevelt invited her to a premiere of *The Eleanor Roosevelt Story*. Agnes was the only woman to be allowed to imitate the voice of the late Eleanor Roosevelt on *March of Time*.

Invitations from Los Angeles Opera Guild's annual benefit Christmas show at the Beverly Hills Hotel (1964 and 1965). The settings were different, as were the chorales and the casts. The only repeat was Agnes Moorehead doing a reading.

The following is a menu Agnes saved from Ross Hunter's Shangri La Supper Dance at the Rainbow Room, 30 Rockefeller Plaza, following the world premiere of the film musical *Lost Horizon*.

Hors d'Oeuvres

CHO CHO	SCALLOPS	TINY DRUMSTICKS
Steak strips coated with sweet-sour sauce on skewers	Marinated in lime juice served in sauce	Deep fried served in apricot sauce

DEEP FRIED SHRIMP	RUMAKI
Covered in Oriental Rice-style noodles	Chicken livers and Water chestnuts in bacon

Entrees

OPAR AJUM
Chicken with almonds and tamarind

PATJERI NINAS
Braised lamb shoulder with pineapple

GULAI UDANG DENGAN LABU KUNING
Shrimp and Zucchini Curry

TOURLOU
An assortment of vegetables with cinnamon

AN HORIZON BOUQUET
Assortment of exotic fruits and sherbets

COFFEE   TEA

Yes, there are blessings, too, with all the invitations galore!

Although there was no date above, it must have been about 1972 or even early 1973. For Agnes telegraphed a friend: "After closing *Don Juan in Hell*, remaining New York for R. Hunter's *Lost Horizon* premiere. Then jetting London for film. Thence to Jacksonville April 7th for Festival. Back to California for *Gigi* rehearsals."

On television, Agnes once did the life of Wanda Landowska, an unpublished journalist and later harpsichord artist. There were fine notices about her performance. Scores of letters poured in, including a touching one from a girl harpist with the pit orchestra in *The Sound of Music*. No wonder she was awarded the coveted human relations award of B'nai B'rith.

There was a beautiful Easter card from the Burt Lancasters among her mementos. Debbie Reynolds sent her a card from Las Vegas (April 1967):

Dear Sister Cluny [from *Singing Nun*],
    Thanks for sweet wire on your old pal's birthday.
                                    s. Deborah

Madame Shirley Saint wrote from Paris: "Miss our wonderful talks."

Greer Garson sent her a tiny night-light. "Try this little night-light for a tiny glow in your glamourous dressing room. Big hug. As ever.   s. Greer Garson"

Someone at Berea College in Kentucky sent her a copy of a poem entitled "High Flight."

Notes of thanks received from Dan Duryea and Mrs. David Selznick (Jennifer Jones).

90

Liz Montgomery wired her at some distant place February 19, 1965: "Schedule prevented my being there. Thanks for your willingness to stand in. *Fly* home as soon as you can, but do take an airplane this time. Much love to you.   s. Liz"

People wrote her constantly about their aches and pains. Perhaps this was because of her roles in many movies. Nevertheless, she would take the time to reply because she never for a minute forgot or neglected her fans.

Someone analyzed her handwriting once: "You are a person of refined tastes and are warm and generous. You are an energetic, persistent and sensitive woman. Finally, you are cultured and have a creative mind." That she did.

Another fan wrote:

Miss Moorehead:
You're only as pretty as you feel and with so many people loving you—you can't help but feel beautiful. Thank you for being the fine lady you are.

Orson Welles' daughter Beatrice once wrote her from Spain (April, 1967): "How I wish you'd come to Spain. If you do my friends would be isterical [sic]." (The letter was typed.) It was one of the secrets of her charm that she appealed to old and young alike.

Dr. Edgar Mitchell of the Noetic Science Institute, Palo Alto, wrote August 21, 1973, "During my flight with Alan Shepard on *Apollo 14*, I was indelibly impressed with a perspective of our planet that is different from one we usually consider. I have reflected upon the incredible panorama and turned my attention to inner space. Could you join me in this endeavor to pursue further this subject?"

One of her favorite bits of philosophy was, "The soul of a thing is the thought, the charm of the act is the actor." She loathed the ugly, nihilistic destructive theater which was being so often foisted upon the public.

Often backstage she would get into a religious or philosophical discussion, not because she wanted to proselytize but just to converse on something higher than the usual gossip.

After one such session, this note was received. "You asked me to define 'love.' How's this? 'Living with and striving toward increasing compassion and truth.' " She really did get some creative thinking across to others.

In our talks we were constantly discussing the fact that there is never any freedom without discipline of some sort. If you do not learn to control you emotions, you become a slave to them and hence your every mood can untrack you.

She loved to repeat in every interview and, after a while, in most conversations when asked about her profession, "You need the courage of a general under fire, the strength of an Amazon, the hide of a crocodile, and the patience of Job."

When people would twit her about some of the raggedy roles she assumed, she was quick to rejoin, "They could yank my teeth out if it would be good for the part."

Joe Pasternak sent out the following instructions regarding the 37th Annual Oscar Awards in 1965: "It is vitally necessary to smooth running of the show that all nominees occupy the seats designated for them. If you are not seated as indicated, the TV camera will not be able to find you at the proper time."

Scores of wires poured in from all over the U.S.A. after she lost the award for her brilliant efforts in *Hush, Hush, Sweet Charlotte*. One said, "We prayed, crossed fingers, even lit candles." Another, "You were so elegant, beautiful, charming and all the things you are, that I cried."

One interviewer divided her comments as: "Agnes is Performer, Perfectionist (up at 4:45 checking set lighting, etc.), Preacher and Philosopher."

That Agnes was a philosopher was evident from all who ever conversed with her for any length of time. Here are a few culled remarks regarding her craftsmanship philosophy.

"A true actress compliments, never competes."

"I've been offered parts I won't touch. I'm not interested in putting audiences in the gutter. If I can't contribute to something good, something imaginative and creative, I'll stay home instead [as opposed to working or going on tour]."

"There must be glamor and mystery where stars are concerned. At one time, I was against their conducting radio tours behind the scenes which showed how they made various sounds. They destroyed the magical illusions."

She liked to remind people that the reason she preferred fantasy to reality was that she was brought up on the Andersen and Grimm stories.

As I've interviewed people the length and breadth of the United States regarding Agnes, certain words repeatedly appeared. They were: "always stunningly dressed," "impeccably groomed," "poised," "forthright."

One of the nicest things I learned about Agnes' effect on persons was told to me by Judge William Eubank of Arizona Appellate Court. He said, "I've seen her for so long in the movies and on television that I count her as among my friends, even though I've never had the pleasure of meeting her." She must have affected many this way.

Arlene Dahl, in an issue of the *Herald Examiner* in 1964, said:

Agnes Moorehead said on advice to young actresses, "If you are interested in and dedicated to making motion pictures, diversification is more important than being attractive in every role. But I don't practice that in the theater (stage). When I'm on stage, I try to be as attractive as possible.

I tell the young aspirants to be immaculate and to keep that young fresh look about them. Don't mask it with makeup when it isn't necessary. Always walk like princesses, proud of their abilities. Develop imagination because if their thoughts are dull, their voices will reflect it. I tell them that to become important to others, they must make themselves interesting to others, each in their own individual way."

One of her long-time friends, familiar with her multifaceted career spanning all possible entertainment media, said of her:

"Agnes' flights of fancy were forgivable because she lived an 8½-dimensional life. Why, once when she was in New Orleans, she discovered an antique store which was still holding stuff she'd picked out on the trip before. She had made the usual deposit down and then completely forgotten it."

Moorehead magic could be either witchedly wicked or saintly sister as when she portrayed a nun.

Don't take my word for it. Chaplains wrote from all branches of the service thanking her for her inspiration and unfailingly adding, "Your father would be proud of you."

Dwight Newton (of the San Francisco *Examiner*, March 8, 1963) wrote: "I don't want to sound blasphemous, but I think Agnes Moorehead can create more excitement with her voice than . . . with her voice and body combined. I'm not saying that just because Virginia Graham said recently that Agnes made Virginia think Lionel Barrymore never died. That voice! That crackling, snapping, sinister, paranoic, paralyzing voice, which captures your attention. She conveys authority, panic, distress, . . . anything she wishes to convey."

Another of her famous preachings about the younger actors and current plots went something like this: "Today by the end of most stories you have to see an analyst. As to young actors, they want to start their careers backward. They expect to start at the top. The problem of the acting profession is really the problem of the generation. It's militant, rationalizing and insecure. Such things rarely sponsor great dignity and respect. One practically has to be a wandering minstrel ready to dash to far-off sets in distant countries. But, there's always hope that the theater can be cleaned up and get some dignity into it to touch the human heart as it always needs to be touched.

13

ABCs—Animals, Books, Cooking

As I said, when at Villa Agnese, she loved to paint, putter, garden a bit, and do household and home chores.

Freddie Jones told me: "If she was going out of town, she'd call the dogs in and pet them and talk with them patiently, explaining how she had to go away. 'Be good girls,' she'd say. 'And above all, take good care of Polly and Freddie.'

"If she went out of an evening, the dogs knew she would call them upstairs to say good night when she returned. She would stand at the head of the stairs at the back stairway and greet them as she came in. They thought it was heaven itself to be able to go upstairs. It was a real treat. They sure liked it.

"She preferred phoning to writing. She would ring us up long distance and her first words always were, 'How are the dogs? Do they miss me? And how are you?' in that order. We never minded it." The black French poodle's name is Dusa. She is the mother of the apricot poodle called Sara.

Freddie and Polly were with her for over twenty years. At first Freddie was the only live-in housekeeper. When joined by Polly, it had become only too clear the house was too big for one assistant. At first Freddie became upstairs person, especially responsible for dressing, clothes, and upstairs housekeeping. Polly was downstairs and did cooking. However, as the years passed and they became used to total routines, they shared duties so that each knew how to cover for the other if illness or other interruptions occurred.

Agnes' favorite recreation was to attend fine movies and outstanding plays, especially when in New York City. She was a movie buff, and she never could get enough of good stage theater, either.

Her favorite vacation routine was to go on a ship's cruise or to be able to take a long voyage enroute to either movie sets or other theatrical business. She took the *Queen Mary* to Europe in 1961. She traveled extensively by ship to Greece, Egypt, and Israel in 1963. Even when traveling, she would make the most of the opportunity to attend plays, concerts, or add to her library and antique collection.

Next, after oceangoing ships, she loved to ride trains. She took trains whenever possible. One could stay a very private person while traveling even cross-country on the train. The bedroom or drawing room compartments on the Pullmans were a delight to stars who sought to preserve their privacy. They could read, work puzzles, sleep, and doze to their heart's content. Meals were brought to the compartment. It was quite a perfect way to travel, Agnes used to say.

She liked to walk, for a purpose. Sometimes when the girls would drive her to the Beverly Hills Hotel, she would say, "I think I'll walk back. It'll be easier for everyone. And the weather is so nice."

Freddie said: "She often mentioned how serene it was at the farm. Once the farm was ready for her, she would beat it there just as fast as she could. It replaced ships, trains, and everything as a private place. Once she stopped me at what I was doing and said, 'Freddie, don't you ever listen to silence?' That one threw me, and I said, 'Well, no, no . . . I never have.'"

We happened to be sitting just beneath the huge super-imposed gold-leaf cupids framed about the mirror above the fireplace. Continuing, Freddie said: "For instance, the cupids came crashing down at one of the parties she was giving. Everyone supposed it would be impossible to resurrect them. At the very next affair, they were restored in fine shape to their former setting. A guest who happened to have been present at the near debacle observed the restoration and said, 'Why, Agnes, where did you get those restored so beautifully?' She answered, 'Freddie and I put them back together.' They didn't want to believe her. She persisted. She liked to challenge herself."

I noticed there was a fresh fruit and vegetable portable truck that called mornings up and down their street. I asked if they patronized it by any chance. "Oh, no. When Miss M. was here, one of us drove her down to Farmer's Market on Third and Fairfax. She preferred to pick out the week's supply herself personally. If she was going to be gone awhile, she would come back with a tremendous stock to be frozen and used as needed."

What were her favorite preparations? I mentioned her telling about Northern fried chicken at the farm. Freddie said, "On rare occasions that she fixed a meal, her favorite was trout, which she prepared with a conglomeration of grapes, almonds, and herbs. Oh, and sometimes she liked to fix lasagna.

"Incidentally, in addition to enjoying buying fresh foods at Farmer's Market, she always had us drive her to a place on Alameda Street each pre-Christmas season where they bring the new cut trees. She delighted in choosing and picking several trees for her annual Christmas bash. Nothing but the best for her guests. She was like a child decorating the trees, too."

One of the rarest antiques is just inside the massive front door on the right wall. It is a funeral wreath made in England by families too poor to send flowers to a service, so they would sew beads as flowers and present it to surviving mourners.

Freddie informed me, "Agnes enjoyed setting the table herself whenever she entertained, especially at Thanksgiving, Christmas, Easter, or special guest dinners such as those with friends from abroad. She not only used all sorts of original place marks but would actually set the silver service herself. It added hominess to Villa Agnese.

"She painted the chandeliers in the entrance hallway. Had them removed to the garage and went right at it. She hand-painted the chests of drawers, including sprinkling them with powder to give a more homey effect. It was her personal touch which can still be felt throughout the rooms and halls of her Beverly Hills home."

Generally speaking, her library seemed to divide itself into the following categories: humor, mystery, religion, drama, biography, and then the broadest possible range of reading. I noted that she often picked up secondhand books while on numerous tours. Many had bookmarks as if she had never completed them, because she was interrupted on tour, came back, and had new assignments or simply never got back to them.

She must have been very fond of the late Robert Benchley's books, because she had over a half dozen of them—*Benchley Beside Himself, Inside Benchley, The Early Worm, After 1903—What?* and more.

The same could be said of Thurber. She had most, if not all, of Thurber's books. One of them, *The Thirteen Clocks*, is inscribed to Agnes by Charles Laughton:

> To a pure artiste
> To a beautiful creative soul
> To a kind, good lady
> A Lavender Queen
> Best ever in Fairy Tales
> My eternal love and admiration
> s. Charles Laughton

Then, in *The Thurber Album*, which includes "Lavender with a Difference," Agnes had written numerous markings for speed emphasis, and added: "Learning how to do a thing is the doing of it, and as my father used to say, 'I am buying some sandpaper to sandpaper my soul,' for the tour that is looming ahead (*Fabulous Redhead*) hoping that I can in some way follow in Charles' (Laughton) wake trying to reach man's heart."

Tucked away in one of the volumes were notes of portions of *Sorry, Wrong Number*, written on St. Francis Hotel, San Francisco, stationery. All creative travelers write on whatever is handy at the moment.

That Agnes was a mystery lover goes without question. It fits every facet of her personality, even to that of being a very private person. Bernstein's *The Search for Bridey Murphy*, Butler's *Kiss the Blood off My Hands*, Chandler's *The Lady in the Lake*, Collins' *The Woman in White*, Crime Club books, Graham Greene books, and a complete eighteen-volume set of Edgar Wallace books were but a few of her wide variety of mysteries.

Her personal religious philosophy was such a dynamic part of her life one would expect to find religious books throughout her library. Both fiction and nonfiction religious books were sprinkled throughout. Auchincloss' *The Rector of Justin*, C. S. Lewis books—including a science fiction book—and books by Peter Marshall, Frank Laubach, Norman Vincent Peale, Emmet Fox, Hurlburt.

Professional books galore lined her various library shelves— especially biographies of great entertainment leaders. There are three on her favorite, Ellen Terry. *The Art of Mime*, by Irene Maurer, happened to be near a painting of Marcel Marceau. The biography of Cedric Hardwicke had comments to Agnes "whose bark has inspired some of my most exalting moments in the theater, my affectionate greetings; here's to more Don Juans. s. Cedric Hardwicke."

In the upstairs library just off the main living room, there are many sets of great books such as those by Sir Walter Scott, Charles Dickens, Edgar Allen Poe, Shakespeare, Alexandre Dumas, Mark Twain, Jules Verne, Joseph Conrad, Guy de Maupassant, Oscar Wilde, Oliver Goldsmith, Robert E. Lee, George Eliot, and Arthur Conan Doyle. Also on the shelves were a book on the queens of England and *The Theater* 1902-08, 1927, 1930, among others. *The Drama*, which covered drama's history in the Orient, Greece, and France through the ages was also included. Naturally there were books on ballet and on art through the ages.

Poetry? Auden, Blake, Brooke, Frost, Nash, Parker, Milton, Masefield, and Millay.

Because of my long association with Pearl S. Buck I was happy to find many of her books. Of course, there would be

Dragon Seed, since she enjoyed being in the movie so much. Out of her sixty-five movies, she had one set of eight pictures of her many parts. Her part in *Dragon Seed* is one of the eight pictures.

Some other favorite authors through the years deck her various shelves: A. J. Cronin, Sholem Asch, Taylor Caldwell, Dorothy Canfield Fisher, Truman Capote, Edna Ferber, and Lloyd Douglas, who wrote *Magnificent Obsession*. There were two copies of Galsworthy's *The Forsyte Saga*.

I looked over several mysteries by Erle Stanley Gardner and Levin's *Compulsion*, on the Leopold-Loeb case.

She must have been fond of Lewis's *The Big Four* (biography of Huntington, Stanford, Hopkins and Crocker). It looked much read. Walter Lippman's *U. S. Foreign Policy*, Sartre's *Age of Reason*, Thomas Wolfe books and many by Saroyan exemplified how universal were her reading tastes.

There were several author's inscriptions to her personally, including Harold Lamb's in *The March of Muscovy*, Gavin Lambert's in *The Slide Area*, and in a first edition of Maxwell Anderson's *Elizabeth the Queen*.

Since Laughton mentioned her fondness for fairy tales, there were over two dozen copies of Oz books. Cecil Beaton's *Fair Lady*, and J. M. Barrie's collected works were there too. An 1832 copy of Fielding's *The History of Amelia*, *Mary Poppins*, and books by H. Allen Smith, Sagan, and Salinger were scattered among the shelves.

Martia Leonard had inscribed in *The Moving Finger Writes* (1946), "from one Dona Ana to another." Apparently she had once played the part too.

The rumpus room was a hodgepodge of magnificent clutter. Parts of it seemed like a jigsaw puzzle because everything fit in perfectly, as a whole.

Throughout the room were many inlaid wood and ivory tables. Brass tables, too, abounded.

There were antique chairs and reading stands—some real treasures.

Scattered here and there were zebra pelt rugs.

There was a Chinese footstool.

Two of my favorites were an ancient world globe built on its own stand and an elaborate wooden birdcage in the shape of the Milan Cathedral.

Two large ceramic elephant end tables, similar to those at the farm, stood near the marble fireplace with its huge brass andirons. They in turn were surmounted by grotesque medieval figures.

On various tables were old radio sets, an antique Victrola, as well as ancient ceramic figurines.

The black upright piano with matching harp had its strings intact (unlike the ancient harp in the upstairs library).

There were several small plain richly upholstered chairs in green and pink.

There were busts of Schiller, Shakespeare, Lessing, and Beethoven.

Numerous sketches and line drawings lined the walls. Above the great sofa was a painting of Marcel Marceau. Just beneath were antique handmade puppets. Currier and Ives also decked some walls.

A massive antique gilded table with a marble top held many pictures of her friends in show business, as well as animal miniatures of which we know she was most fond of collecting.

Magazines? In addition to every possible trade paper that one would expect one of her professionalism to subscribe to, there were: *Town and Country, Harper's Bazaar, McCalls, Good Housekeeping, Ladies Home Journal, Saturday Review, Vogue, Coronet,* and *Readers' Digest.*

Movie scripts of *Johnny Belinda, Caged,* and *Singing Nun* were back in her private office.

Her much-worked jigsaw puzzles were boxed in stacks in her private office.

I was particularly pleased to run across John Houseman's autobiography, *Run Through,* which he autographed for Agnes on September 3, 1972, in Los Angeles. It was beautifully inscribed "For Agnes with love and admiration — building and accumulating during a very long and inspiring association. Above all, with thanks for her incalculable advice and help with staging and production of *Don Juan in Hell* in its second time around tour."

Agnes and John had been associated in the very beginning of the Orson Welles *Mercury Theater of the Air.* Howard Teichman recalled an anecdote of Mr. Houseman and Miss Moorehead reaching way back to the thirties. It had something to do with one of her numerous radio parts. Considering it was the depression years, and it involved money, all the drama was not always on the air.

In a small frame on her personal desk in her private office, there was a poem dated June, 1973. In the light of what was soon to happen, the words are particularly significant.

> Deep into the now
> forever awaits
> be still
> and remember . . .
> the great knowledge will emerge
> and your soul will take wings
> for He takes great joy
> in the singing of your heart.

14
Versatility

We have seen this extraordinary woman's profile in radio, movies, television, stage, and readings. Now we will mention a few of her further conquests in what has to be the most incredible entertainment record in the history of the American theater.

Just as few realized that Agnes was a pioneer in many radio serials and a pioneer in many television parts, practically no one realizes she once appeared in vaudeville with long-forgotten Baker, Bottle and Company (or something like that).

Fred Carmichael said: "Somewhere back in the twenties Agnes not only appeared in Vaudeville with Phil Baker (and the above-named company) but actually got away with doing a simplified version of the bumps and grinds in Boston, of all places. How did she manage it? Because she was Agnes Moorehead, that's how. As she said, she did it like a lady."

So, add vaudeville to the above-mentioned five major forms of entertainment.

Next came recordings. One of her most popular albums was *The Psalms of David*. Her recording of *Sorry, Wrong Number* was a hit. Goodness knows how many albums of *Don Juan in Hell* with the cast of Laughton, Boyer, and Hardwicke were sold. Agnes also did *Nancy Hanks, Barbara Fritchie*, and *Common Heritage*. Thus we learn she added a seventh field of entertainment.

The jacket on the *Psalms of David* says:

> Agnes Moorehead, master of her craft, is a dramatic star of seemingly unlimited abilities. Her awards in the media of drama have been many and varied, including the New York Film Critics Award, Academy nominations and the International World Award. Miss Moorehead's classic recording of *Sorry, Wrong Number* is used for many studies in many universities and colleges throughout the country.
>
> Her nationwide tours of *Don Juan in Hell,* the recent play *The Rival,* and her brilliant one-woman show *The Fabulous Redhead* will long be remembered.

The artist's rare gifts of talent and deep spiritual faith give new beauty and meaning to her interpretation of The Psalms.

Would you believe she also did voice-overs? In a movie entitled *Charlotte's Web*, she was the voice of the stuttering goose. Debbie Reynolds was the voice of the spider, Tony Randall was the voice of the rat, and Henry Gibson was the voice of the pig. This was her eighth field of entertainment.

From my research of Agnes Moorehead's touring in many stage plays, including *Don Juan in Hell*, and her tremendous one-night show across many many years, I believe her to have set a never-to-be-duplicated record of appearing in more cities in more states than any performer, actor, or actress, in American theatrical history.

When we add her personal appearances, I'm sure she set a never-to-be-equalled record as a trouper. For example, look what she did as judge of American GI plays for our Army:

Itinerary - May 2-13, 1968:
  Dep. London 1115 2 May
  Arr. Berlin 1340 2 May
  Dep. Airport for Hqs. 1430
      Hqs. 1500 - 1520
      Hqs. Brigade 1530 - 1535
      Berlin Hilton Hotel 1615

      Armed Forces Radio 0930 3 May
      Armed Forces TV 1100
      Hotel 1200 - 1300
      Checkpoint Charlie 1330
      East Berlin and Checkpoint Charlie 1630
      Hotel
      Outpost Theater 1930 - 2330

      Hamburg, Bremerhaven, 4 May
      Hamburg, Frankfurt, 5 May
      Worms 6 May

Heidelberg 7 May
Goeppingen 8 May
Munich 9 May
Verona 10-11 May
Verona-Munich 12 May
Frankfurt 13 May

Daily parades, judging plays, visiting clubs, and a host of public appearances. All this in twelve days!

There is mention of her appearing at Hermosa Beach, California, at the *1912 Days*. Stuart Whitman was grand marshal of the parade. Agnes was honorary mayor.

She also appeared at the famous New York *Herald-Tribune* book and authors luncheon that was held on April 23, 1952. (She probably was touring with *Don Juan in Hell* at the time.)

While in *Bewitched*, it was requested that she attend the annual Akron, Ohio, Soap Box Derby.

Her campus visits were always over-scheduled, but never was a complaint heard from Agnes.

While appearing on the Buffalo telethon for children's philanthropy, she was heard over the radio February 25-26, 1967, over stations in Jamestown, Lockport, Olean, Niagara Falls, Batavia, and Dunkirk. At this time, one of her fans wrote, "I watch you on 'Andora [sic].' "

At the tenth annual Thalian Ball in October, 1965, she helped raise one hundred thousand dollars for emotionally disturbed children by giving readings with Raymond Massey, Angela Lansbury, and Sam Jaffe. Debbie Reynolds and Donald O'Conner were co-hosts of the ball.

C. Gershenson told me: "Agnes cheerfully appeared at a *Fiddler on the Roof* benefit party in November, 1971. Despite an eye infection, she was the hit of the evening. What a trouper."

Phil Breedlove, Jr. told of seeing Agnes at Palm Springs on various tours. Her involvement in good causes always impressed him.

While doing personal appearances, there were always the

inevitable interviews. Many complained that she would talk about Laughton, Welles, and Gregory instead of about herself. This was her way of keeping her private life separate from her public image.

James Corcoran of the Hollywood Bowl Easter Sunrise Service wrote her in January 1972: "Would you please favor us *again* with your unforgettable rendition of 'The Master Is Comin'? Bishop Sheen will be the speaker. As in the past, you will be furnished with a limousine."

Francis Lederer wrote her in August 1972: "Your rendering of the poem as a tribute to the Lunts was one of such supreme craftsmanship, skill and exquisite taste that it will remain forever in my memory as one of the finest performances I have ever seen. . . . I never cease to be thrilled by something as exquisite as you have offered. Alas, such artistry is only too rare."

Agnes served as grand marshal of the San Jacinto Christmas parade in 1971. In 1968, the Los Angeles Opera Guild starred Agnes in their annual Christmas program. She gave special Christmas readings. So, whether it was for Christmas, Easter, for charity, or whatever, she always gave her best. No one who ever heard her forgot how fine and how great, how exquisite her best was.

She served during these years on the Arthritis Fund Drive Committee and the Glendale, California, Charity League Board. She was also honorary chairman of the Illinois Cancer Society.

Anne Baxter thanked her for serving on the National Cystic Fibrosis Foundation. Glenn Ford wrote to thank her for serving on the 1967 Eye Dog Foundation.

Agnes never neglected her religious duties, no matter how busy she might be. The pastor of the Hillside Baptist Church at LaMirada, California wrote her in March 1967:

> The Holy Spirit used you mightily to speak to the hearts and minds of our people. We praise God for your love for His Son and your *willingness* to share your faith with us.
> s. D. E. Reiter, Pastor.

Helen Blair of Longview, Texas, told in a letter in 1968 of a long evening's discussion on church and Christianity.

There is a reference in the same period of weeks to her attending the Monte Carlo Film Festival and appearing at Cacoctin Mountain Park in Thurmont, Maryland.

She appeared at the sixteenth annual Variety Club Telethon at the Allegheny Center Mall in Pittsburgh.

A student in Ontario, Canada, after seeing her in *Don Juan in Hell*, wrote: "You're a very special lady. Please take care of yourself. When you act, you look so beautiful and oh, that glorious voice. My friends only see the perfected look of haughty disdain which you have made so famous in so many movies and plays. I close my eyes, hear your glorious voice and see the radiance that permeates your whole being when you are on stage."

On the more humorous side, a friend wrote, "Why must you always undermine my hysteria [*hysteria* was crossed out and *vacillation* was written in] with your logic?" I have rarely met anyone so devastatingly logical as Agnes was.

I've frequently mentioned the avalanche of letters she would receive after just one appearance on a television show. Some beautiful ones were received following her Red Skelton and John Gary shows.

As with all famous people, she was not spared, either, when it came to being confused with someone else. There was one letter addressed to "Ms. Natalie Moorehead," which found its way to her.

Her kindnesses when she visited campuses, even writing to thank student hosts and hostesses, caused them to reciprocate with innumerable letters to her. The little more and how much it is; the little less and how it wiles away.

As if she wasn't busy enough with all the versatile entertainment media phases, Agnes had long dreamed of her own acting school. I found a reference to her Saturday teaching schedule, October 18, 1969 to June 27, 1970. She would rent a studio and devote her precious Saturdays to her school. Eight A.M. was given over to techniques. Shakespeare was at either ten, eleven, or at twelve-thirty. Apparently they took early lunch breaks. One forty-five was screen plays.

There is mention of Al Hirt's daughter attending, and, at perhaps an earlier form of the school, there is mention of Mia Farrow.

The Moorehead acting philosophy did not ever include the idea that acting could really be taught, but the rudiments and the techniques of acting could at least be interpreted. Speech, body movement, integration, interpretation and reading techniques were very essential. In addition, there must always be something *more* than personality. That indefinable something —call it spirit, call it psyche, call it the *summum bonum,* whatever—it is a certainty that Agnes Moorehead exuded it.

I like to think that perhaps one of Agnes' greatest personal achievements in *her* sight was something that very few people ever even knew about. Because it was connected with the production of *The Life of Christ*, it must have brought her much personal enjoyment to have been chosen to tutor Jeffrey Hunter in his vocal attempts to somehow simulate the very voice of Jesus. How that must have seemed right and proper to Agnes. How closely she must have felt to her earthly father, let alone to our Father, as she endeavored to refine and spiritualize the voice of Hunter so it could be a sterling credit on the film.

Agnes was a writer, too. The only thing she ever had published follows exactly as printed in *Guideposts,* August 1965.

MY FAVORITE SCRIPT
by Agnes Moorehead

I was asleep in my home in Beverly Hills, California, the other night when the telephone rang. It was my mother, in Wisconsin.

"Who," she inquired, "was Moses' mother?"

For the moment I'd forgotten the name "Jochebed" but believe me I never will again. Mother often checks up on me by phone this way, just to make sure I'm not neglecting my Bible.

She needn't worry. I may forget a Biblical name occasionally but I'll never forget that I need this Book every day of my life. For me, as for my parents before me, the Bible is as current as today's newspaper. When I was small I loved the story of the Israelites in the desert. My father was a Scottish Presbyterian minister and from the pulpit he would make very real the cloud by day, the fire by night, and the manna that God sent from heaven. This was more than ancient history to Father; it was a description of God's caring here and now. He firmly believed that God has a sign in His sky for us this very day, and guidance for us tonight, and manna for every need of our lives.

How I tested these passages during my own desert days in New York City! I'd gone there with the goal of every young actor: to make my way in the theater. To make my money last, I ate almost nothing: hot water for breakfast, a roll for lunch, rice for dinner. It was hungry work, making the rounds of casting agents, mile after mile on the unyielding sidewalk, and I used to wonder fervently just how God was going to provide manna in this man-made wilderness.

At last came the day when I was literally down to my last dime. I stood in front of an automat gazing hungrily at the plates of food behind their little glass doors. The trouble was that one of the agents had given me clear instructions, "Phone, don't come in," which meant that five of my ten cents would have to go into a telephone box instead of opening one of those little doors.

With dragging feet I went into the drugstore next door and changed my worldly wealth into two nickels. I shut myself in the phone booth at the rear of the store, inserted one of the precious nickels—and then waited in growing alarm for the operator's voice. Half my fortune was in that phone, and nothing happened—the coin was not even returned to me! I jiggled the hook. I pounded the box, but it held tight to the coin that would have bought me a big white roll—and a pat of butter on the plate beside it. As always when I let myself think about food, a kind of desperation seized me. I thrust two fingers into the coin return, clawing the cold metal sides of the tube. They closed on a piece of paper.

Though I didn't know it then, I had stumbled onto a familiar racket of those days. Pay phones were built in such a way that a piece of paper inserted from the bottom would trap the money in the chute. All I knew was that as I drew out the paper, a little river of money streamed into my lap: dimes and quarters as well as nickels. In all, when I had finished my incredulous count, I had $4.25.

I knew, of course, that the money belonged to the phone company—and I paid it back with interest as soon as I could. But I never doubted, also, that this money was manna direct from heaven. The oatmeal and rice it bought lasted until I got my first part.

Does God drop manna through phone boxes? Of course. Anyone who spends much time with the Bible recognizes humor as one of the surest signs of His presence. And the Bible-reader also comes to accept this loving involvement with the details of our lives as a fact about Almighty God. The non-Bible-oriented mind reels before a fact like this. That the Force which flung out the universe should also stoop to feed sparrows is too much for our unaided intelligences, and so we devise descriptions of the universe other than the Biblical one, mechanical and naturalistic theories that better fit our own man-sized understanding.

These philosophies are particularly hard on young people. I can still remember what my father said when I first encountered them in college. I would come home puzzled by a lecture or a book that flatly contradicted the Bible-centered world in which I'd been raised. Father never attacked the argument itself. He would simply ask one question:

"What interest does it pay?"

The thing that you believe in, he used to say, is the greatest single investment you can ever make. Before you invest, he would tell me, check on the kind of return you can expect.

Father believed in the Bible, in every word between its covers, and for him the return was joy, peace, victory, a serene and unassailable love of God and men. This didn't mean that he understood every word of Scripture.

"When I come to something I don't understand," he would say, "I leave it for later. Perhaps I'll have to leave it till this life is over. But I don't doubt it. In my hands I hold a holy thing."

I had dramatic proof of this when I did a one-woman show recently in Israel. After the performance an official of the national museum asked me if I would care to see the Dead Sea Scrolls. For an hour and a half I wandered through the vaults where these treasures are kept, marveling at the scholarship which assembled them. But the true marvel, the revelation which sends you to your knees, is that the "Isaiah" so recently unearthed here is the "Isaiah" in your own King James Bible. Every actor knows how hard it is to be sure exactly what Shakespeare wrote, less than 400 years ago. Different manuscripts of his plays disagree. But in thousands of years of travel, turmoil and translation, nothing has been lost from God's word.

My father is dead now. He died in his pulpit at the close of a Sunday sermon some years ago, and I like to think of him now sitting at the foot of the Author Himself, learning at last every secret of the Book he loved. But the love itself lives on: in Mother, in me, in the congregations he served.

The Bible is the first thing I read every morning of my life, and the last thing at night. Most mornings now I have to leave the house at 5:30 for a six o'clock call at the TV studio. This means that my Bible reading time comes at 4:45 a.m., but I would no more skip it than I would skip dressing. Again at night, when I've read the next day's script, I open the Bible. There I find rest for my weariness, strength for the job ahead, a pillar of fire to guide me through the night.

111

Part Three

For *Margery Stover*
     Vic Stover

Interlude ————————————————

What have we learned about Agnes to this point? My wife says: "Agnes Moorehead, the regal realist, spent a lifetime making the world of make-believe seem like reality for her audiences.

"Even as a small child she created new characters at whim by answering her mother's 'Good morning, Agnes' with a matter of fact 'I'm not Agnes, I'm Maryann.'

"Agnes always prepared in depth for any situation. But all the preparation in the world couldn't prepare her against life's exigencies. She was severe with herself but ever forgiving of others.

"Each new challenge or experience would find her as totally prepared as possible.

"As a drama student she would spend long hours reading various types of material aloud, changing inflection, accent, and tones. She would memorize dramatic passages, practice facial expressions and gestures before her mirror, able to let herself go in recreating a character or a part in a manner in which she could not let herself go when being herself.

"In later life, after her reputation became established, she would find it easier to create the character of Agnes Moorehead, actress, for the world to see and would allow even less of her inner self to public view.

"She used all her experiences and observations of other people to improve and perfect her own life. Probably her most common thought was 'When I do that, I'm going to do it this way.'"

Summarizing what we have learned about Agnes I would say: She was first, last, and always a superb actress—beguiling, bewitching, demure, strong, confident—yet sometimes afraid—funny, comical, a wit when she wanted to be, a very serious person, sharp, testy, snappy, a great lady, courteous, kindly, thoughtful. She gave and gave and gave. Though basically strict, she could be lenient. She had a definite sense of humor, yet she was decidedly intellectual, philosophical; homey, but could sweep onto a floor with the awe of an Empress. She liked animals, played Scrabble, liked mysteries, ditto puzzles, enjoyed good theater and movies. She was a religious person who loved America. She was a very private person yet anything but a shrinking violet.

15
The Farm

Margery and Vic Stover are the caretakers of Agnes' farm down among the foothills of southeastern Ohio. The original land deed is signed by President John Quincy Adams. The farm has belonged to some part of the family for all these years.

Agnes had long wanted to acquire total ownership. She had wanted to build a new place down in the woods since 1942. I called it "New Place" to distinguish it from the "Homestead" up on the hill. It was finally begun in 1969. It was finished in 1972. It covers about 7500 square feet.

All I could think of as I visited New Place, walked where Agnes had walked in the primeval-like woods, was "If there is a heaven on earth, it is here, it is here."

In an original first-time interview, the Stovers were most helpful. Margery Stover told me: "Agnes used to spend her summers here when her grandparents were still alive. During the Depression she would ride a horse into Cambridge, which is a long hard ride.

"She used to like to sit on the steps of the Homestead and dry her hair, and comb and brush it by the hour. She had a fantastic dislike for wigs, probably because she often had to wear them in movies and television. As she grew older, she disliked doing her hair, so I would help her when she was here."

Since the farm was willed to John Brown University in Arkansas, I asked if it was a working farm.

"Oh, yes," Margery replied. "We have 125 acres in baled hay (80 percent clover, 20 percent legumes). Vic has helped build up a herd of registered Black Angus cattle. You know how fond of animals Agnes was."

I had noticed a beautiful appaloosa mare just over the back fence by the barn behind the Homestead.

"Agnes named the appaloosa Endora. It was a great favorite of hers."

When we held our first lengthy conference inside the Homestead, Margery pointed to three beautiful colored decanters and said, "Those were our last Christmas gift from Agnes in 1973." She continued, "Her last visit here was October of '73. We knew she wouldn't be here for Christmas because of touring with *Gigi*. With the constant arrival of Christmas packages, we asked what to do with them. Agnes said, 'Please let them wait until I get here, whenever that is.' "

Sensing I was anxious to see New Place, Margery and Vic accompanied me by car. Just by the narrow lane from off the road leading past the Homestead stood a huge oak tree. Margery grabbed my arm and said, "Stop a minute." Then she told me that one time when Agnes was arriving, in addition to all the other treats the children and adults had prepared for her homecoming, they tied a huge yellow ribbon on the old oak tree. She was so happy with the reception.

Proceeding slowly down the little lane that Agnes love to walk upon, the Stovers pointed out dogwood, redbud, white

117

trilliums, blood roots, spring beauty, lilac trees, yellow violets, and satiny purple violets. "Vic, Sr., would pick a small bouquet of fresh violets and hand them to her in the mornings."

There were fruit trees of every description indigenous to Ohio. There are the hugest beech trees I have seen anywhere in the United States. They are of tremendous girth and reach far higher into the sky than any beech I have ever seen.

Agnes had such magnificent respect for every living thing. The whole place is so naturally beautiful, all I could think of was Albert Schweitzer's reverence for life.

Margery said: "Agnes used to say, 'It's not God's will to ever stop learning all the time. We must never stagnate.'

"In the four years it was my privilege to know her, I came to understand her philosophy about getting along with others. She took what was good about them, even if she disliked their ideology. This was evident from her good works for others, whether Jew or Gentile, whether liberal or conservative. You know how fundamentalist she was religiously and how conservative politically. Her living her philosophy of seeking good in each was Americanism at its best, let alone living her religion.

"She used to repeat, 'We can't live another person's life. Some people just don't want to let anyone live their own life.'

"She was a most disciplined actress in her art and never known to give a bad performance. But would you believe she was a compulsive shopper?

"She especially loved good soaps. Soaps in every size, shape, description, smell, color. Do you know there are over forty Christmas boxes waiting to be opened for the Homestead, New Place, Stovers, and other persons?"

It seems appropriate to insert at this point a part of a letter I received from Margery Stover in December 1974.

For weeks now it has seemed so odd not to be receiving the dozens of boxes which would arrive, some to open, some not to open. What a lovely time she had in all the shops. She often said, "This is my only joy on the very lonely tours—to shop." As Vic and I unpacked the Christmas decorations this year, there are several things she sent to use that sent me into a tearful afternoon, and again, I had to *convince* myself that she was really gone.

There is a set of little angel lights, and a string of circus cars with an animal in each one. There are a big stuffed Mr. and Mrs. Santa that stand up on the floor or a table. Last year at this time we were calling each other at least twice a week. She wanted to get to the Farm so badly.

I would tell her what we were going to decorate and what I was baking and cooking. Some of the airlines were having strikes and were cutting flights because of the fuel shortage. As gas was scarce she was afraid to take a chance.

I can hear her say to me as clear as day, "Don't open the boxes from such and such, they can wait until I get there. Then we will have Christmas no matter when it is."

So it ended up that Vic and I sat on the closet floor the night she died and opened the boxes. There will never be another Christmas that I will not think about that and the shopping she did—ill as she must have felt, only weeks before her final stay at the Clinic. I miss her so.

Agnes and Margery had many things in common in addition to their interest in religion and their philosophy of Americanism. Both grandparents of theirs were farmers. Marge liked to shop every bit as much as Agnes. And they loved to watch old movies.

Margery said: "Some people can get to know one another as well in four years as some in forty. People just couldn't accept it that we hit it off so well. For instance, when she was at New Place, she'd ring me up here at the Homestead and say 'Guess what's on as an old rerun tonight?' Then she'd rip off the year it was filmed, the cast, and general plot. When she asked, 'Can you leave the family a bit and watch it with me?' I'm so glad now that I never let her down.

"Another thing we had in common was the belief that the country is God's church. Everything on the ground, in the trees, on the bushes, and a-wing is part of the living sanctuary. We both loved twilight, eventide, and the early morningtide. If she came in from a long trip at four A.M., after grabbing a few wink's sleep, she would be out walking and drinking in the beautiful sky, fresh air, and all of God's lovely nature bright and early.

"She would say, 'I don't see how anyone can live on a farm and be an atheist. God's creative work is everywhere.' "

When I walked through the woods on the old wagon path to the open fields high on a windy hill, I was never so aware of walking in someone's footsteps. It was as if she walked right there with us again!

I had felt her living spirit in the New Place. She had left her imprints there. The only other home in which I have ever experienced this living-spirit-of-owner after someone had departed was FDR's place at Hyde Park. I felt his presence still there. Walking and sitting in New Place, strolling about the spacious grounds and down through the woods was an actual spiritual experience. It was aided by the fact that everything had been allowed to be as close to its naturalness as can be. I have never seen such glorious beech trees, never walked in such sublime serenity and quietude. It is a worthy memorial to a great lady, a fine Christian woman.

Margery told me: "Like so many generous souls, some thought she was tighter'n bark on a tree. The nearer truth was that it was easier to get ten thousand from her for a worthy project than ten dollars for a handout.

"She was never Greta Garboish as a few thought, but she believed that her life offstage was different, and she aimed to keep it selective. She gave liberally, as you know, to personal appearances, which are a form of staginess. But when she was to herself, she preferred to do her own thing.

"Do you know what she'd do at the shoe store when she

bought a new pair of shoes on the road? She'd have the old pair shipped home to the farm. When we'd open the box, there'd be a good laugh all around. . . . the truth was she loved to wear old ones comfortably about the farm.

"Vic and I believe we are two of the luckiest people in the world to have been let inside her private shell. We have been so enriched by her personality and character. She will never die where we're concerned. Not a day passes but we recall something she said or did.

"When she was told the New Place was finally ready, she and Freddie's husband, Rochelle, arrived with two truckloads of furniture. To our surprise, not even a toilet was working. She was nonplussed at first, but not for long. You know how fast she could overcome any obstacle, it just made it more challenging."

I asked Margery if she ever got to make any trips from the farm with Agnes.

She replied: "When the rare occasion offered itself to travel with Agnes on either a speaking or reading engagement, I would drive her to her destination. We always stocked up on buttermilk. When we arrived at the motel, we would submerge it in ice, prop ourselves up, and watch old television rerun movies. It was more fun!

"I recall one trip to Milledgeville, Georgia. It was a real knee slapper at times. The motel sign said 'Vacancy.' We stopped. The man there said, 'We ain't got no room.' We replied, 'The sign says so.'

" 'Nope. It don't work none.'

" 'Can you help us find a place nearby?'

" 'Try (name of broken-down hotel in nearby town.)'

"While we were talking to the old codger, a drunk tried to pick us up. 'Howsabout a drink of cold be-er,' he said.

" 'No, thank you,' Agnes said very formally.

" 'Don't ya know the geese are flying South? That's why there ain't no rooms.'

"Agnes said, 'This is one goose that ain't flying South

because of the snow up north. I'm on business.' With that, we left.

"We arrived at her place to speak and discovered a beautiful old restored mansion. As she was going into a reception, a gentleman said to her, 'I sure enjoyed your lecture last night, ma'am.'

" 'Sorry,' Agnes replied, 'I just arrived. It couldn't have been me.'

"He persisted, 'Well, then, who are you?'

"She screwed up her mouth in her famous way and raised her eyebrows in the gesture she was so renowned for, but before she could answer, he said, 'Now, now, Miss Moe-head, don't you git agitated none.'

"We went in one place and the host said, 'Aren't you—'

" 'No,' she said, 'sorry, I'm just made up this way.'

"One man insisted we stop at Tallulah Gorge on the way back. As we gazed upon it—after reaching it with considerable difficulty—Agnes said, 'Humpf, first time I ever knew Tallulah had her very own gorge.'

"We went in another place and every time the table was touched, it spilled coffee because it was lopsided. The coffee was fetched at once, pronto. We never did get waited on. While waiting, Agnes took some sugar packets and balanced the short side of the table. Waited some more. Got more coffee. Never did get to eat, so finally left.

"There was one restaurant we ate in that a little girl came up to Agnes and said, 'Aren't you Endora? May I please have your autograph?'

" 'Certainly,' Agnes replied. As she handed it to the little girl, the girl started off in a rush. Agnes reached out and grabbed her. She put on her witchiest look and said, 'And what do you say now?'

" 'Thank you, oh, thank you.'

"Agnes let go her grip and the little tyke really took off then."

After being led around the spacious grounds of New Place

and having interviewed the Stovers the night before, I went inside the next morning.

It is beautiful—beautiful in a most unusual way. One can tell every bit of tender loving care went into the planning and construction of New Place. It's a privilege just to see it!

The parking for cars is in a circular driveway. There is a large two-car garage with a passageway or patio connecting to the main house. We entered through the kitchen. It is large, functional, and modern, but done to a turn in an old-fashioned way. It's the size kitchens used to be in the old homesteads and farm houses. No family room or such at the end of the island counter. Just a great big old kind of comfy kitchen with every appliance imaginable but done to taste and necessity.

One then passes through to the great livingroom. High beamed ceilings, very similar to Villa Agnese, but otherwise no mimicry or aping of the Villa. Rather a considerable attention to keeping New Place to its own individuality. There is a grand piano.

Her precious Maud Adams award is atop the piano. The award is an indescribable modern art piece representing free spirit. It is presented to an American woman who has made outstanding contributions in performing arts. She was introduced as "America's most honored actress."

Upon accepting, Agnes said: "I accept this award for my work which requires *agony* and *resolve*—not for profit or fame. But to create out of certain materials something that didn't exist before. An actress must have discipline and be dedicated to her work. Acting is not just a gifted art but must be developed into a craft that requires training, scholarship, learning of technique, and acquiring of experience.

"A character isn't a static thing and can't be built like a wall. The hardest job is to be sincere and *detached*. Young actors and actresses think all they need is sincerity—this is not enough. One of the ills is today's pornography. Sexual and social passion are both deeply self-indulgent and theatrical people have basic instinct to be self-indulgent. But they should realize that the theater itself is not immortal. There were centuries when civilization had no theater. TV and picture magazines are causing people to lose their capacity to listen to words or follow ideas. This is not true of great theater which envelopes the audience and makes it involved in what is happening on the stage."

There are some elephants and knight's masks pieces similar to Villa Agnese. Otherwise antiques take over instead of Mediterranean villa style.

The elegant but functional fireplace at one end of the living room dominates the room. Many huge sofas, plus several groupings of chairs and pillows, round out the room. Near the fireplace is a handcarved Austrian cherry bric-a-brac shelf that is indescribably beautiful. There is a huge brass angel in this room plus a beaded coral agglomerate.

Among the elegant clutter of books, knickknacks, and antiques, I observed several angel paintings, a pewter angel, a little loving cup with the words "World's Greatest Actress."

There was a miniature gilded director's chair, miniature dolls, and more miniature chairs. Above the one bookcase was a picture of Debbie Reynolds and Agnes with their director in the middle. Each actress was jokingly holding a dagger pointed at the director.

We've already established elsewhere that she liked animals — living or effigies. I noted throughout the sitting room off the bedroom a huge bullfrog with a top hat, a monkey satyr, owls, swans, leopards, ducks, dogs, fish, and ceramic elephants from Asia.

The foyer of New Place has an Indian charcoal brazier, wall-to-wall Greek white shag rugs, and an antique ceramic umbrella holder.

Marge Stover told me that Agnes ran extension cords everywhere. She just somehow never got accustomed to using switches.

Agnes' mother's bedroom off the foyer is all done in pink. There are even pink wicker chairs, a pink wicker clock, and pink candle holders.

The lavatory is antique porcelain from Europe with gold-plated faucets, whose handles are fish shaped.

Agnes' bedroom is Moorehead Mauve. Lilac, purple, and mauve abound. Even the doorknobs are pastel originals. The towel rack has two hands gripping the rod to hold towels. The chandelier is a cluster of lavender grapes.

She loved collages and oil miniatures. They are all through the bedroom and sitting room. The *Prayers of Peter Marshall*, which Marge gave her one Christmas, is next to the bed on a little table.

Marge said, "We sort of played a game with her Bible. She would always leave a place marked for me to read after she left. The last time she was here last October, she left the Bible opened to Psalm 96:1-16, which was appropriate to harvesttime in the fall. There was always a pen and one of her lavender hankies in the spot she wished me to read."

She loved to philosophize about her beloved religious beliefs. Agnes said: "I never knew of a will that any attorney drew up that another smarter attorney couldn't break. The only unbreakable will is the Legacy of Christ."

Another favorite quotation of hers (not necessarily original) was: "The atheist doesn't find God for the same reason a thief doesn't look for a policeman."

Marge recalled that Agnes' favorite book of the Bible was Proverbs. That figures.

Marge and she often discussed her childhood memories of formal worship, stained-glass windows, the music, the ritual. I chimed in that she and I often discussed her growing concern about the influence of the occult and Satanism. Marge replied, "True. We often talked about it, too."

Because she did not want to miss out on worship while on tour or studying lines, she subscribed to many religious tapes.

I told Marge how Agnes and I often discussed the idea of Protestantism being a separate faith. Each of us had noticed that in hospitals and other institutions that we visited—Agnes to perform and make personal appearances, myself in the tour of duty as minister or counselor—we were often misinformed that someone was a Protestant when they happened to be of no faith whatsoever. It didn't bother us except for the fact that the administrators were confused. They wrongly assumed that if a person wasn't a Catholic or a Jew, they must be a Protestant. Hence they called them such on entry cards.

As anyone knows who has thought about the matter, Protestantism is a way of life, a faith, with roots in both Catholicism and Judaism and yet quite separate. It is a faith of its own and should never be confused with labeling people solely because they aren't something else.

Agnes and I had many discussions on this. We had each run into it so many times. At first we each thought it was a mistake on the part of the institution. Not so. It's ignorance, and mainstream Protestantism itself ought to assert itself to correct the misapprehension. This is not to denigrate either Judaism or Catholicism. It is merely to correct an often-made mistake.

Another anxiety of Agnes was that early religious training of so-called free churches is not only neglected, but the Bible in all its fullest literary beauty is unknown and unappreciated. She was in absolute horror of the religious illiteracy of children and of the lack of word usage. If the youth do not learn to communicate better, how can they be expected to understand great literature?

I neglected to mention earlier that as one enters the great living room, one is confronted with a most striking portrait of Agnes styled as Queen Elizabeth I. It was from a movie entitled *Story of Mankind,* filmed in 1948. Agnes appeared as Elizabeth Rex in it. The beautiful portrait hung in a Chicago gallery until 1973 when it was removed to New Place. It is six feet by four feet, in oils.

As Marge Stover spoke about Agnes both at the Homestead, at New Place, and in the car, I kept hearing certain words repeated: "gracious," "human," "fun," "mimic," "regular," "homey," "relaxed," "happy," "contented," "generous."

Before New Place was finished, Van Johnson was a guest at the farm in 1971 while appearing in a play in Cincinnati.

I had discovered several times that Agnes would research a part in a movie or play before she attempted the characterization. What I didn't know until I visited the farm was that, as Marge Stover said, "She was always anxious to add to her store of Americana. Whenever the setting was in a new locale or historical, she was anxious to add to her storehouse of America. No wonder she was such a solid American. Her Americanism was manifested in many ways.

"Did you notice the American flag waving from the flagpole in the circular driveway as we came in? It was one of the last things she did, that is, order a bright new flag for the new pole."

I heard many anecdotes about Agnes and pigs—yes, pigs. She liked them the most of any animal. She thought they were the most misunderstood.

Marge related: "We were stopped by a service station one time and a load of pigs was parked next to us in a huge truck. Agnes started mimicking the pigs. They snorted right back. They each kept it up until the truck pulled away. Then Agnes said, 'Sometimes I think I should become a vegetarian because I like animals so much.'

"She could mimic frogs to perfection. We called it her 'frog bit.'

"Once she arrived in the middle of the night at Columbus airport, in 1970. 'Please come get me,' she phoned. We arrived at 7 A.M. All she had was the clothes on her back and an overnight case. 'Where's your luggage?'

" 'It's at the baggage turntable.'

"We walked over. First I grabbed ahold. Couldn't even budge it. Then Vic grabbed ahold. He could barely move it. We called for a Skycap. Together, the Skycap and Vic managed to wrestle the bag to the car.

" 'What on earth you got in there?' we asked. 'Doorknobs,' unabashedly came the reply.

" 'Doorknobs? You've got to be kidding.'

" 'No, I figured with the shipping costs so high the only way I'd ever get those knobs here was to use all my allowable allowance plus overcharge for poundage. So, here we are!' "

The library at New Place is a treasure for one interested in books. The first to catch my eye was *The Life of Isabella Stewart Gardiner* of Boston. Agnes once thought she would like to do a story of her fabulous life. I noted another book about Mrs. Gardiner's famous home, which is now a noted museum in Boston.

Burke Davis was a favorite author of Agnes. She has several autographed copies of his books such as *The Gray Fox, (R. E. Lee), They Call Him Stonewall, Jeb Stuart,* and *The Summer Land.* The last named is a quite comical novel about North Carolina tobacco growers.

She admired Jessamyn West books. As we noted at Villa Agnese, next to humorous books, her favorite light reading was mystery books. She really went all out for Agatha Christie stories, (especially her Hercules Poirot).

Two personal friends' biographies of Joan Crawford and Ruth Gordon were next to her reading chair.

Agnes liked biographies. *The Dream King* (Ludwig of Bavaria) was a favorite of hers. *One Hundred Great Lives* sat next to it.

I noted *A Treasury of Italian Villas* had a prominent place in the library at New Place. There was also the *Encyclopedia of Paintings of the World.* Add Gilbert and Sullivan (plus the World Library) and one realizes her broad diet of reading.

The *Complete Works of Shakespeare, Longfellow's Poems, The Secret of Santa Vittoria* were closely shelved together. Also, Zondervan's *Answers to Biblical Questions* and lots of children's books.

The children's books were for any visitors. Marge said, "Agnes liked to keep up on what was being put out for the children." This certainly is in keeping with her interest in better homes and families as bulwarks in American moral life.

For what was to turn out to be her last visit to the farm, Margery Stover prepared a sumptuous feast. They had baked sugar-cured country ham, mashed potatoes, vegetable soup, potato salad, homemade raisin bread, cinnamon rolls, black cherry jello, and German chocolate cake.

Young Heidi Stover once asked Agnes if she could really do all those things that Endora did on *Bewitched*. Agnes replied, "Only on Thursdays," then added, "after I've stirred the cauldron."

"You mean Sundays, don't you?" the child asked. That's when their part of the country got the program.

At New Place there were additional awards, other than those at the Beverly Hills home.

I noted that the Massachusetts Chamber of Commerce complimented her on being a Great Living Bay Stater, since she was born in the Bay State.

The State of Texas made her an honorary citizen on February 6, 1971.

The Thalians awarded her a certificate on December 14, 1967.

The Hollywood Headline Club gave her their 1971 Award: "To a talented lady and lovely actress who has displayed amazing versatility and outstanding acting through an exciting career."

The Hollywood Bowl Easter Sunrise Service cited her on its golden anniversary in 1970.

The University of Wisconsin Greater Los Angeles clubs cited her in 1972 for her contribution to the entertainment field and distinguished professional achievement.

As we were riding to New Concord, Margery recalled Agnes' lifelong addiction to the famous washboard sidewalk at Muskingum College and what Agnes would call the "goofy" roads in her childhood farm days. (I believe she meant the Pinchot roads.)

Margery continued: "Agnes claimed her first performance was out at the old picnic grounds." Marge and I walked out there on a hillside overlooking a magnificent view. I could imagine Agnes walking in the silences of the great woods of towering beeches. The birds were singing, we saw humming-birds, noted woodchuck holes. There were wild grapevines throughout the wooded area.

"Agnes always kept a salt block in the yard for deer and any other strays." As we walked back from the old picnic grounds, Marge regaled me with some travel anecdotes.

"Do you know she once hitched a ride at one o'clock in the morning from San Francisco airport to the intown Hilton? The driver was going to let her off down the street. She said, 'At this hour of the morning?' Gallantly, the driver deposited her at the very door. It was a semitruck!

"Once we were bringing a U-Haul truck with antiques to the farm. We parked at one of the poshest restaurants in Columbus. They were expecting Agnes to leave in the customary Hollywood-type limousine. Instead, she climbed into the rent-a-truck and gaily waved to gaping admirers as we pulled away.

"You know she preferred auto, train, or bus, I presume. She would only take a plane if absolutely necessary.

"Has anyone told you about the time they were doing *Gigi* in Detroit and the drapes fell down? She ad-libbed for five to six minutes until everyone could get collected."

"Were her fears that patriotism in home and family was at the bottom of the totem pole justified?" I said to Marge. "We often discussed that."

"She admitted she was a flag waver just as she was never ashamed to practice good manners, grace, and etiquette," Marge replied. "Her heroes were men like General McArthur, Ronald Reagan, and John Wayne. Did she ever tell you about the time they were filming *The Conqueror* in Hungary with Wayne? Times were pretty awful there, so she would sneak any clothing she could to the small children who crowded around the filming cast."

I took a very reluctant leave of New Place. I had noted a beautiful edition of G. C. Morehead (no relation), the Kentucky painter who is known as "the artist of property." His book was crammed with beautiful historical buildings. I've seldom seen such an exquisite volume.

As we drove away from the circular driveway with Old Glory proudly waving in the breeze, I noted some beautiful shrubs and flowers. "Vic, Jr. helps with these," Marge said. "As she left on her final visit, we have often recalled that she stooped down to Vic, Jr. working on flowers, and said, 'Could you give your make-believe-aunt a kiss good-by?''

16
A Dear and Valued Friend

Agnes' last words to Paul Gregory when they met for what was to be the final time in New York City were "Religion softens the edges."

After I returned from the long visit to the farm, where I was favored by Margery and Vic Stover's original interview regarding Agnes, Margery sent me the following:

Here are some notes Agnes wrote on Bible Study (not necessarily original):

The Bible was intended to be more than a handbook of Divinity. True believers hold that all Bible doctrines are of men, but constitute the positive thinking of God, himself. The mind of man must be indwelt by the Holy Spirit or the contents cannot be discerned or understood. The truly wise man does not criticize the Bible, but lets the Bible criticize him. It seems to be that latter day Christians have taken to believing that it is by grammar and commentary that they can understand the New Testament. Nothing is understood without direct spiritual illumination. The true believer prays, "Open thou mine eyes, that I may behold wondrous things out of thy law." Ps. 119:18.

A Christian should have complete faith and trust in his Saviour, his God. Faith is the assurance of things hoped for—the evidence of things not seen. Tears of sincere grief over sin lead to a saving trust in God. Without faith repentance recedes into indifference.

The Old Testament is the covenant of God made with man about his salvation before Christ came.

The New Testament is the agreement God made with man about his salvation after Christ came.

In the Old Testament we find the covenant of law.

In the New Testament we find the covenant of Grace, which came through Jesus Christ. One led to the other.

I am a Bible searcher because I am a Christian. I believe the Bible. I am a searcher also in that I must continue to search my own mind on whether I have interpreted properly the true meaning of the scriptures. One revelation leads to another. Many religions and churches have their own interpreters and interpretations. One must never be led from the true word. One must only search to understand the true word. Romans 6:17-20 (cite) and Matthew 24:55 - "Heaven and earth shall pass away, but my words shall never pass away."

Say to yourself, "I am here not to be a teacher or to preach but only to witness." Become a searcher!

The record of God stands in spite of the vicious attacks against it through the ages. The Holy Scripture is indestructible. Ps. 12:6-7.

Saving faith is believing with the heart. Heart in the Bible stands for feeling, thought and will.

Saving faith is our need for salvation, and earnest desire to be saved. Faith that He died for our sins brings pardon.

Faith that He rose again brings deliverance from sin's power. This, too, must be heartfelt faith and heart-full faith.

Results of faith? We are saved through faith. Salvation

132

is a free gift. Faith appropriates to itself this gift freely offered to all. God's love is a blank check. We are free to fill in the amount.

God's inscrutable judgement is deeper than can be penetrated by man. Paul says that those who raise themselves above the heavens in their reasonings utterly forget who and what they are. Therefore man is made to set himself above God. It is intolerable to man that God's power and word exceed the capacity of his own mind. He will grant to an equal his mind and judgement. We cannot question God or examine Him.

Other books are soon out of date but the Bible spans the centuries. Most books have to be adapted to age, but old and young alike love this book.

The Bible was written by God through good and wise men. Bad men could not have written it, for the Bible is a good book. And, as we know, fresh waters do not come from a salt fountain. Bad men would not have written it, for it condemns sin and sinners. Wicked men would not condemn themselves. Good men would not have written it and then said, 'God wrote it.' They would not then have been good men. It was not written by good men for deception, for good men do not deceive. Hence the only one left who could have written it was God.

The best and wisest people (not necessarily intelligent) of the world have always believed it.

Further proof: It is a pre-written history of a nation, the Jews. None but god could have written such an accurate history years, and in some cases, hundreds of years before the events happened.

The Bible describes exactly, precisely with uncanny exactitude the Jewish people as they are today.

Right things are the best things to pursue and do, by the nature of their being. A thing is right to do because it contributes the most constructive possibility. It is right because the consensus of the best authorities have endorsed it. It is the right course because it is the most spiritually remunerative of any possibility. Therefore, knowing the right, there isn't any alternative because right is that which is most spiritually advantageous and all souls seek betterment. The purpose of life on earth is that the soul shall grow. So—*grow* by doing what is right.

Marge wrote:

These thoughts are so much proof of her deep and abiding faith, that all who read them cannot help but find the desire for a more sincere search of their own beliefs, and of where they are going in today's world. My own deep faith is what gave Agnes and myself another channel of communication. Her faith helps sustain me through the grief of losing her in my own life, I have been much enriched and fulfilled by her love and friendship. Perhaps this is what God wants our life to be—one friend to another. It may be that the death of a friend and loved one, only makes us better understand what one person can do for another. That you can enrich and expand your own life by accepting love and friendship as well as giving it. Accepting what others give with deep appreciation, and accepting them and understanding them as they really are and of course, hoping they will do the same with you. When we lose someone we always wonder why him or her, when there is so much evil still left in the world? We always plan on a tomorrow instead of living each day as though it were our last. When there is no tomorrow for a loved one we are shocked into realizing we had better come to terms with the fact we don't know and aren't meant to know when our last day will be. I truly believe God's purpose in bringing Agnes into our lives was to help make us better by her example. The fact that she accomplished this is further proof to us. Perhaps we were sent to her when she needed faith restored in the honesty and reliability of people after so many delusions and setbacks in her plans for expansion of the Farm. We can only hope that we helped fulfill a dream, and gave love and friendship as we had received in turn.

People are so easily forgotten as the years go by, but here, she shall always live. We cannot go through a single day without feeling her presence. How thankful we are that we let her know how much we loved her and thought of her, even though she had won fame and fortune she let us come inside her very private person and we hope she was the better for it.

Perhaps, unknowingly, Agnes has brought us all into new friendships.

One of the favorite utterances I came across regarding religion that I know was a favorite of Agnes' was "Anyone who contends that God is dead only confirms that He existed."

She used to say often, "I cannot conceive of a life devoid of His Presence. My love for others, my fellowmen I trace to my friendship with God. We are all part of the 'main' as John Donne said. God taught me this. I sing his praises forever."

Just as she was able to discuss her faith with persons all throughout this land and others, I came across a note from a friend in San Francisco after her final visit there with the *Gigi* cast. It was not signed. It said, "I was particularly delighted when you told me yesterday religion was the only motivation for carrying on your work as you had done. Thank you, too, for your words, 'We owe a duty to our Creator to work hard to make His grand provisions for mankind available to all under our free enterprise system.' I am fortunate to have been able to talk with you and be inspired by you."

I believe I omitted the fact she always drank Sanka. This was part of her discipline and dedication to using her fullest faculties. If she ever smoked, she had long since dropped it as not suitable for her philosophy and religion. She was ever concerned about young people, whom she felt were "tending too much toward self-destruction. Their sit-ins, dropouts, cop-outs and love-ins were nauseating demonstrations" in her book. This no-nonsense attitude permeated her whole way of life whether at work, at Villa Agnese, or on the farm.

As I have been rethinking our long conversations regarding religion and her personal philosophy, I just recalled something that Cesar Romero shared with me but I had neglected to mention. He said that Agnes called him long distance the day that our men first set foot on the moon. He said she was visibly agitated. He wondered at the time as I have since, if this was a premonition on her part of the troubles about to descend on us with Vietnam, the presidency, and the recession. Or was it an uneasiness prompted by her conservative religious beliefs that somehow this was not perhaps necessarily in the best Biblical tradition? (For my part, I will never forget the reading of the astronaut from Psalms as he beheld the universe from a position never before trod by mankind.)

Inside her front door she kept a constant supply of fan pictures for handing out to the steady stream of visitors who would ask for such. It was her firm belief in importance of fans that prompted this. She said, "It is the principle that led me to idolize Dame Ellen Terry, the famed English actress whose theatrical life spanned sixty years. While I was in my teens I wrote to Ms. Terry. I still treasure her letter and the picture she sent me. Her thoughtfulness added to my incentive to go on the stage. You see, I can understand and appreciate fans because I, too, was a fan."

Shirley Eder wrote in her new book *Not This Time, Cary Grant* (Bantam, 1974) of being able to watch Ginger Rogers in a rehearsal in Detroit of *Pink Jungle*, produced by Paul Gregory, because Agnes Moorehead, "whom I knew," was kind enough to arrange the visitation.

Harris Vincent of Salt Lake City told me at Castle Hot Springs, Arizona, that he listened to Agnes give a dramatic reading on Art Linkletter's *House Party* somewhere back around 1971-72. What was extra fascinating was that the reading was from the Beatles' song "Eleanor Rigby." Harris said, "I shall never forget her interpretation and insight of her reading. Even *it* was drama at its finest."

Although I have previously mentioned Joseph Cotten's interview, I was thrilled the night he appeared on television recently for a special award to Orson Welles. Cotten said, "Orson practically forced us onto radio via the *Mercury Theater of the Air*. Orson literally pushed us onto the stage via famed Mercury Players. But most of all, he shanghaied us [himself, Agnes Moorehead, Ray Collins] off to Hollywood to make *Citizen Kane*."

Agnes and I shared two very positive ideas. Agnes said: "No matter what our profession, our vocal ability plays an important part." And "The purpose of theater is to entertain. Acting ought to be to amuse with contentment. It ought to excite with a capital *X*. To have great theater, it must be from the heart."

Agnes personified and exemplified her philosophy whether on stage, screen, radio, readings, recordings, or what. Her heart and her head, her body and her soul made her the entertainer extraordinary.

Lucille Ball lived diagonally across from, and down the street in the same block with, Villa Agnese. I have mentioned elsewhere that Lucille and Agnes were often Scrabble partners. Miss Ball wrote me a note which I think is the finest way to conclude this book.

Agnes was a dear and valued friend — an elusive one — because she was forever helping someone in our business. She was one of the greatest dramatic teachers and comedy advisers in our profession. Her timing was impeccable. One of the greatest things she gave her pupils and friends was the knowledge of the discipline needed to pursue any phase of our beloved show biz. I admired her greatly and miss her every day.